*"God does nothing but*
*in answer to prayer."*

**John Wesley**

"As the debates raged, I heard a common theme in the voices of conservative and progressive delegates: desperation."

"The thing about dumpster fires is that in order to extinguish one, you must spread all the burning material out on the ground and let it sit there for a while."

"Hard conversations should only happen in these contexts, not in the political body of General Conference where the clergy delegates across the world only see each other every four years."

"Stepping down that hill toward the parking lot, I was overwhelmed with grief for what had become of the church into which I was ordained."

"Here's the rub. The General Conference asked the Council to lead and yet they did not agree with the recommendation of a majority of the bishops."

"I say these things not as a skeptic or to deny scriptural authority, but as one who consistently fails to be faithful."

"We are a deeply divided Church, and it would be naïve of me to think that we will soon settle our disputes."

"Whatever decisions we did or didn't make in St. Louis were going to leave a permanent mark on our church."

"I have wondered why so many UM's have been silent while this virulent campaign of control over our denomination has marched on."

"Delegates from former Soviet Union nations and the Philippines spoke similarly. Culture in all three continents is influenced by Islamic prohibition of homosexual lifestyles."

"The present crisis has brought us up short. Our "realism" doesn't look so smart anymore."

# Where Do We Go From Here?

Honest Responses From Twenty-Four
United Methodist Leaders

## Compiled by Kevin Slimp

## Contributors

| | |
|---|---|
| Jorge Acevedo | Donald Haynes |
| Sydney Bertram | William B. Lawrence |
| Sharon Bowers | Sharma D. Lewis |
| Wil Cantrell | Laquaan Malachi |
| Kenneth L. Carder | M. Douglas Meeks |
| Kenneth Carter | Rebekah Miles |
| Alex da Silva Souto | Chris Ritter |
| Talbot Davis | Don E. Saliers |
| Katie Z. Dawson | Kevin Slimp |
| Bob Farr | Amy Valdez Barker |
| Thomas E. Frank | Laceye C. Warner |
| Erin M. Hawkins | J.J. Warren |

Market
Square
BOOKS

# Where Do We Go From Here?

*Honest Responses From Twenty-Four*
*United Methodist Leaders*

**Compiled by Kevin Slimp**

©2019 Market Square Publishing, LLC
books@marketsquarebooks.com
P.O. Box 23664  Knoxville, Tennessee 37933

ISBN: 9781732309296
Library of Congress: 2019940427

Printed and Bound in the United States of America

Editors: Kristin Lighter and Kevin Slimp
Assistant Editor: Sheri Hood
Post-Production Editor: Ken Rochelle

Cover Illustration ©2019 Market Square Publishing, LLC

**Where noted, Scripture quotations are from:**

# Table of Contents

# Preface
# Kevin Slimp

When my friends kept asking, "Where do we go from here?" I decided the church deserves a response.

On March 3, 2019, I showed up at Middlebrook Pike United Methodist Church as I do on most other Sundays. At approximately 9:00 a.m., my son and I moved the four-foot-long conference tables to make room for the class members. He alphabetized the name tags, while I placed Bibles around the room and scribbled a few notes on the whiteboard.

I had planned a lesson as usual, this one from Donald Haynes' *A Digest of Wesley Grace Theology*, which we had been studying since the beginning of the year. My strategy was to approach class in normal fashion. This meant members would wander in beginning around 9:30, tell jokes and swap stories, then settle down for prayers and announcements at 10:00.

Our class has been around for almost twenty years and it's somewhat of a microcosm of The United Methodist Church. Our youngest members are twenty-four-years-old. Our oldest are in their eighties. We have conservatives, liberals, and everything in between. Every so often, a youth walks in and joins us. We have married members, single members, gay members, widows and widowers. We've had Catholics, Baptists, Episcopals, Muslims, Mormons, Pentecostals, Quakers and others wander into our group and call it home for a while.

Our class is a large class in a mid-size local church. On a given Sunday, our normal attendance hovers around thirty-five.

I believe it was Cindy who was the first to ask upon entering the room. The question seemed to be on just about everyone's mind. During prayer time, someone brought up the General Conference and mentioned we should pray for our church.

Noticeably absent that Sunday were about a dozen of our usual attendees. It was early March, after all. Maybe it was a cold day, keeping people home. I don't remember.

1

I often wake early and such was the case the following Monday morning. Retired United Methodist Bishop Kenneth Carder and I had met a few months earlier at a conference event held at Concord United Methodist Church in Knoxville, my hometown. He wrote a few days later to discuss my publishing work and soon we were having frequent early morning chats on Facebook Messenger.

During our Monday morning chat, I asked how his Sunday School class responded to the decisions of the recent General Conference. I learned there were a lot of similarities between the class he teaches in South Carolina and my class in Tennessee.

I wasn't sure how to approach the subject, but finally blurted out, "I'm thinking about publishing a book called *Where Do We Go From Here?*"

My idea was to contact twenty or so recognized leaders in the denomination and ask each to write a chapter in response to the question, "Where do we go from here?" I hoped Bishop Carder would let me know if he thought it was a bad idea.

"That's a great idea," he responded. "Let me know how I can help."

I found Facebook groups of Progressive Methodists, Traditional Methodists and Methodists groups not affiliated with either viewpoint. I created posts on these sites, asking member to send names of United Methodists they would like to hear from on the topic, "Where do we go from here?"

Armed with a list of eighteen names, Bishop Carder and I discussed the list in detail, determining who each of us knew well enough to invite to write a chapter. Later, he emailed those he knew and I sent requests to everyone else on the list. I was surprised when fifteen of the eighteen responded with "Yes."

Along the way, writers would email me with suggestions of other folks who could make significant contributions to the book. Before long, our list of fifteen co-authors grew to nineteen. Just two weeks before this book was scheduled to go to press, I heard from a few of our authors that the book could use even more viewpoints. On Easter Sunday 2019, I wrote to seven more potential authors, asking if they would consider writing a chapter for our book. The catch? I needed their text no later than Thursday.

Four answered, "Yes."

I was pleasantly surprised that bishops, general agency directors, and pastors took time to respond to my question on Easter Sunday.

Kristin Lighter, an editor at Market Square Books, and I set out to gather the manuscripts, do a first-edit of the book, and distribute chapters to authors quickly. Sheri Hood, daughter of Bishop Carder and an editor in her own right, volunteered to help.

With an incredibly tight deadline – a book generally takes a year or more to get to market, and our plan was to release *Where Do We Go From Here* in ten weeks – we didn't waste time.

This book is a labor of love. The authors agreed to donate royalties to United Methodist Committee on Relief. Countless pastors, bishops, seminary professors, laypersons, and publishing professionals pitched in to see *Where Do We Go From Here?* become a reality while its content is still viable.

My sincere thanks goes to Bishop Kenneth Carder, who has spent hours sharing ideas and making suggestions related to this book. The co-authors worked quickly to meet our deadlines. Kristin Lighter and Sheri Hood spent many late evenings scouring the manuscripts of the writers. Before the book is sent to press, Ken Rochelle will go over the entire manuscript one last time – we call this the "post production edit"– for last-minute corrections.

Obviously, the question of where we go from here isn't limited to United Methodists in the U.S., and we hope to publish future books which include responses from members of the global church. For the moment, my prayer is that the words of these writers serve as a place to begin this discussion ... a discussion that won't end within the physical limitations of these 200 pages.

Where do we go from here? I invite you to read the honest responses of my fellow United Methodists. You might wish to use these responses as a catalyst for your own thoughts and a resource for study and discussion.

**Kevin Slimp** is publisher at Market Square Books. For more than two decades he has been a popular speaker at communication, journalism and publishing conferences internationally. Previously Communications Director of the Holston Conference of the United Methodist Church, he has been featured speaker at major religion conferences including The International Conference of Religious Communicators and The International Conference of Catholic Communicators. He has authored or co-authored several books, including *The Good Folks of Lennox Valley* and *Understanding Your Call*.

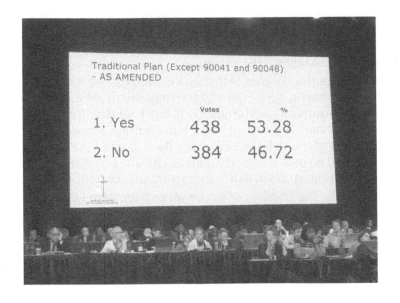

# CHAPTER ONE
# Jorge Acevedo
In the Aftermath of the United Methodist Vote,
There Are No Winners

This past February, the General Conference of The United Methodist Church met in St. Louis for a special called session to address the ongoing impasse in our denomination around the extent of LGBTQIA+ inclusion in our church. In our system of church governance, the only group that "speaks for the church" is the General Conference. This representative body of our twelve million-member global denomination was charged with seeking a way forward.

I would describe the denomination's current position like this. If you could imagine the following spectrum:

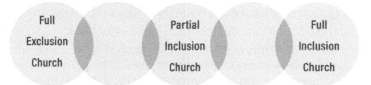

A "full exclusion church" would not welcome LGBTQIA+ persons into church membership or discipleship as well as not marry or ordain LGBTQIA+ persons. A "partial inclusion church" invites LGBTQIA+ persons into membership and discipleship but would not do LGBTQIA+ weddings or ordain practicing LGBTQIA+ persons as clergy. A "full inclusion church" would welcome LGBTQIA+ persons into membership, discipleship, marry them, and ordain as clergy.

Using my spectrum, the current official United Methodist Church position is partial inclusion and has been for nearly fifty years.

## A Way Forward Out of an Impasse

At the 2016 General Conference in Portland, the Conference asked the Council of Bishops to lead us through this fifty-year impasse. They formed the Commission on a Way Forward, made up of thirty-two pastors, bishops, and lay persons to develop potential plans to move us forward in our denominational dilemma. I was selected by the Council of Bishops to serve on the Commission and gave more than one thousand hours traveling domestically and internationally to nine meetings over seventeen months.

The Commission on a Way Forward offered three potential plans to the General Conference to consider: The One Church Plan, the Connectional Conference Plan, and the Traditional Plan.

- The **One Church Plan** would allow for differences in practice within our denomination around performing same sex marriages and LGBTQIA+ ordination based on contextuality.

- The **Connectional Conference Plan** was a complicated plan that would create at least three non-geographical branches based on ideology around human sexuality.

- The **Traditional Plan** affirmed our current position and increased the amount of accountability for compliance around our position.

As a member of the Commission on a Way Forward, I was asked to help make the report from the Commission to the General Conference. After four days of worship and prayer, as well as painful deliberation, the 864 delegates from the United States, Europe, the Philippines, and Africa voted to affirm the Traditional Plan.

As you can imagine, not everyone is pleased with the results. Just a quick look at social media would reveal the pain that many are feeling, especially LGBTQIA+ persons, their families, and allies.

## Differing Convictions: Can There Be Unity?

As a leader in our denomination who has been a delegate to four previous General Conferences, and as an observer of this special called General Conference in St. Louis, I am profoundly acquainted with the brokenness and division of our church. I have sought to be a bridge builder in our church between evangelicals, centrists, and progressives. I honestly struggle with our current "winners and losers" culture at General Conference.

There were no winners this winter in St. Louis, in my estimation. My personal convictions are that same-sex behavior is not God's will for followers of Jesus. The issue has never been a salvation issue for me, but rather a sanctification issue related to same-sex behavior. The question, for me, is not, "Can you be gay and Christian?" I believe the answer to that is, "Yes." The issue before us is, "What does God ask of gay Christians?" I believe a faithful, biblical, and historical response is that God invites all believers to place their sexual behaviors before God.

Having said all of this, faithful, Bible-believing, Spirit-filled followers of Jesus do read scripture differently around these issues. In my estimation, there is no space for arrogance or unquestioned certainty in these painful deliberations. We are not simply talking about an *issue*, but our LGBTQIA+ sons and daughters, neighbors and friends, coworkers and associates. They are children of God and persons of worth.

N.T. Wright, a prominent New Testament scholar, was interviewed by *Christianity Today*. The article asked him about Paul's passion for unity in his thirteen New Testament letters. As it relates to his own Anglican Church struggles with the extent of LGBTQIA+ inclusion, the article stated:

When I ask in particular about debates on sexuality, Wright avoids specific theological pronouncements. He says that "agreeing to disagree" done properly should make demands on people's charity, but never on their conscience. He warns against a dualism that devalues the goodness of creation and a Gnosticism that says "this shabby old body that I have doesn't matter, what matters is the spark of something different which is inside me which tells me who I really am." He adds: "We have to remember that the early church didn't make its way in the world by becoming like the world."[1]

These ethical problems are not simply trivial, he says, but concern what it means to be fully human, living in the light of God's new creation.

"You can't give one-line answers to the so-called moral dilemmas of our day, because you need to take several steps back and say that the way the early Christians approached this is so different from how we do moralism in the early twenty-first century, and if we want to learn wisdom we have to do the hard work of going around that stuff, and not assuming we can either say, 'Silly old Paul, we don't need to take him seriously' or 'Oh yes, it's in the Bible therefore bang, end of question.' It's the Pauline point again: we have to learn not only what to think but how to think."[2]

The bottom line is that this is a very difficult conversation that

---

[1] Hartropp, Joseph, "NT Wright: St. Paul was an 'extremist' who was despair at our church disunity," April 19, 2018, ChristianityToday.com, https://www.christiantoday.com/article/nt-wright-st-paul-was-an-extremist-who-would-despair-at-our-church-disunity/128560.htm.

[2] Hartropp, "NT Wright: St. Paul was an 'extremist' who was despair at our church disunity."

requires deep trust and humility and not simple, "one-line answers." There is a tension to be managed between charity and conscience. People of good faith have differing convictions about the extent of LGBTQIA+ inclusion in the church. Grace Church, the church I love and have served for almost twenty-three years, is committed to continue "to partner with God in transforming people from unbelievers to fully devoted disciples of Jesus to the glory of God." This is our primary mission to all people regardless of age, gender, race, economic status, or sexual orientation. We will continue to love and welcome all to come and follow Jesus.

## Repentance Comes First

One final word. I've argued that the starting place for most traditionalists in The United Methodist Church about our conversation of LGBTQIA+ inclusion is repentance. Over what?

- Repentance of our unkind words and jokes about queer people.

- Repentance of not creating safe places and spaces for queer followers of Jesus to wrestle with the Bible as well as be fully included in the Body of Christ.

- Repentance of our inconsistent sexual ethics, especially around divorce, cohabitation, pornography, and adultery.

- Repentance of our theological superiority and elitism.

- Repentance of our idolatry of certainty.

Then maybe, just maybe, we'll be in the holy space where we can have holy conversations with sisters and brothers in Christ with whom we have huge differences about LGBTQIA+ inclusion.

**Jorge Acevedo** is the Lead Pastor at Grace Church, a multi-site, United Methodist congregation in Southwest Florida. Jorge was the 2001 recipient of the Denman Evangelism Award from the Florida Annual Conference and was a 1996, 2000, 2004, 2008 and 2012 delegate to the Jurisdictional Conference and a 2000, 2004, 2008 and 2012 delegate to the General Conference. He served on the Call to Action Steering Team (2009-2010) and the Commission on a Way Forward (2017-2018) for The United Methodist Church. Jorge co-authored *The Grace-Full Life: God's All-Reaching, Soul-Saving, Character-Shaping, Never-Ending Love* (Abingdon Press, 2017) and *Sent: Giving the Gift of Hope at Christmas* (Abingdon Press, 2015). He also authored *Vital: Churches Changing Communities and the World* (Abingdon Press, 2013) and co-authored *The Heart of Youth Ministry* (Bristol House, 1989). He has also written for The United Methodist Publishing House, Circuit Rider Magazine, Good News Magazine and Our Faith Today.

# CHAPTER TWO
# Sydney Bertram

Clemson University Student Prays,
"Lord, Make Us Whole"

In the weeks following the General Conference decision, I spent so much time thinking that it was hard to get anything done. Scrolling through Facebook, I came across a quote that a friend's mother posted, taken from retired Reverend Eston Williams, declaring, "At the end of the day, I'd rather be excluded for who I include than included for who I excluded."

Yes.

Yes.

*Yes.*

"Open Hearts, Open Doors," we say.

Perhaps not for all.

I am hurt, I am confused, and, in the words of Reverend Williams, I really would "...rather be excluded for who I include than included for who I excluded." If the church takes some parts of the Bible in historical context, considering the biases of its writers, why do we exclude passages about homosexuality from that process? I struggle to understand why we extend the full welcome of the church to women and divorced couples but still shrink back when someone wearing a rainbow stole enters the sanctuary.

Looking beyond General Conference 2019, the issue of biblical interpretation looms large. In this light, homosexuality isn't the most pressing division in the church, though it's certainly the most damaging symptom at the moment. The most pressing division is over interpretation of the Bible, the God-breathed scripture and basis of our faith, that we all love.

We know we are called to be a unified body, but how can we remain unified while we disagree over interpretation of the very book that calls us to unification? Our well-intended reverence for our scriptures places us deep within trenches of opinion and tradition from which we are scared to exit for fear of violating the Word of God. If both sides could climb out into the No Man's Land of admitted uncertainty, perhaps we would find that the expected landmines and barbed wire do not exist. The last time an issue of interpretation such as this faced the global church, Martin Luther penned his "Ninety-Five Theses." In Europe, the centuries following the Protestant Reformation were characterized by religiously motivated warfare, and even today many Protestants I know "just don't get Catholicism" (and vice versa), as if we don't all believe in the same love and forgiveness shown to us through Jesus' crucifixion and resurrection.

Though it seems improbable at the moment, I hope we can skip past the centuries of warfare, today fought with hardline Facebook posts and pointed Tweets instead of swords or mounted soldiers with muskets, and return to doing the work of God in the world. Fearful people hide behind their armor and their keyboards. What do we have to fear? The Lord is on this boat with us.

When I sat down to write the blog post that inspired this chapter, my purpose wasn't to propose a solution for our church. I don't have one, though I hope that by discussing this conflict openly and prayerfully, I can be a part of one. I wanted to share that I was confused, express all of my confused ideas so that I could begin to move on, and maybe share a few thoughts that my readers hadn't been able to put into words.

Two days after I turned thirteen, at my long-awaited confirmation, I made vows in front of my church. First, and most importantly, I publicly professed my faith and desire to serve the Lord. That promise, though sometimes difficult to follow with all my heart, mind, and soul, is uncomplicated; there are few conditional statements to consider. I want to follow God's will. There is no dissonance surrounding that.

My promise to be loyal to The United Methodist Church and strengthen its ministries—a vow I made after promising to serve the Lord—is the part that is proving more complicated at the moment. Thirteen-year-old me, standing between her parents with a flower barrette in her hair, could not fathom the complexities of theology, scripture, and doctrine facing the church.

I didn't realize how much this denomination meant to me until I realized how unsettling it was to feel at odds with it. I was baptized in front of my family's United Methodist Church in Mississippi as soon as my neck could support my head for the pastor to sprinkle water on it. United Methodist summer camp was the first place where I was truly in awe of the Lord. United Methodist churches have welcomed my special needs brother with open arms, creating special Sunday school classes and accommodating my family during services. Reflecting on this, I realize that perhaps I was appreciating of the church what I should have been appreciating of and attributing to God. The church is a vessel for God-seeking people to grow and serve. It is a gift from God, but because of our sinfulness, it can be an idol if we place our faith in the organization instead of its Maker.

*"As I explore my personal call to mission, these questions are increasingly relevant."*

How should I move forward with my new understanding of the church's imperfections? Do I stand up to protest injustice against the LGBTQIA+ community at the risk of weakening the church's other ministries? What does loyalty mean when the church's legislative body makes a decision that, to me, violates Jesus' greatest commandment?

The consequences of a mass exodus from the UMC are grave for millions around the world. In South Carolina, my home conference, what happens to Epworth Children's Home, supported by churches in the conference? To Asbury Hills summer camp, which changed my life and continues to change so many lives every summer? To the Aldersgate Special Needs Ministry, provider of loving homes for special needs adults?

The list goes on, and around the world ministries of The United Methodist Church hang in the balance. Our prayers, presence, gifts, service, and witness are essential to successful mission and ministry. There is no doubt that we are better equipped to do ministry when the Body of Christ is united.

As I explore my personal call to mission, these questions are increasingly relevant. The global ministries of The United Methodist Church do important work in social justice, health, and disaster relief. These ministries exist with the altruistic, ideally agape-motivated goal of both sharing Jesus' message and engaging communities to improve their standard of living. I know I am meant to join with the church to meet these goals. But would participating in this work with The United Methodist Church, through my complicity in the exclusion of an entire group of people from the church, dishonor the message of Jesus and diminish standards of living for LGBTQIA+ people? Conversely, would failing to join The United Methodist Church in its missions do the same against those served by Epworth, Asbury Hills, Aldersgate, and other ministries around the United States and throughout the world?

The problem with Reverend Williams' quote, as visceral as my initial reaction was, is that it fails to recognize that by excluding myself from the church to stand for the inclusion of all, I paradoxically exclude many other people served by the ministries of The United Methodist Church. I cannot assume that someone else will step up and take my place if I leave the church. Every member of the Body of Christ has a role to play. Would failing to tithe, transferring membership, or stepping back from the church unintentionally put more value on the lives of my LGBTQIA+ brothers and sisters than my brothers and sisters who live at Epworth?

I don't know the answer. I don't know how to find the answer. I don't know if there is an answer in this life. However, as I've asked these questions, the church has reassured me. When I say "the church," I don't mean the General Conference. I mean the adults and peers, lay and clergy, from my home church and campus ministry, who have been vulnerable with me. They, too, are struggling with these same questions.

If the twelve million United Methodists around the world join in struggle and vulnerability, twelve million prayers will be lifted every day about the way forward from our "Way Forward." And we know that our Lord is faithful, answering every prayer in time. If we seek God, we will find God waiting for us. We need to be ready to interpret and act on God's will, whether that divine will meets our preconceived notions and personal desires or is revealed in ways we never could have anticipated.

Post-General Conference, I think that I have unintentionally and subconsciously put blame for "our" loss on "them:" the evangelical American churches, the African Central Conferences, and the Philippines Central Conference. I suspect that I am not alone. Our way forward cannot be one of blame and bitterness.

This returns us to the issue of interpretation. If we truly support interpreting the Bible in the context of its writing using the lens of *our* present culture, can we blame people living in other cultures for having different interpretations than we do? When I blame instead of understand, I look past the plank in my eye and focus on the speck in my brother's eye.

While I fully believe that God calls for *all* people to be included in *all* roles in God's church, I have to respect the backgrounds of church members from around the world. In many countries, to be homosexual is to risk imprisonment. In these situations, it is difficult to fathom the church condoning violation of laws rooted in persistent social norms. Adopting a pro-LGBTQAI+ doctrine could also alienate the church from the government. The American principle of separation of church and state does not hold everywhere (or even within the United States), and a government and church at odds could severely disable effective ministry, missions, and humanitarian operations.

To protest that *we* should not be the ones who must split off, that it should be *them*, perpetuates our subconscious feelings of white American superiority. We know that racial and national superiority do not belong anywhere, let alone the church. It is clear that One Church and Simple Plan supporters are in the minority in the global United Methodist Church right now.

Jesus teaches, "Blessed are the peacemakers, for they will be called children of God." (Matt. 5:9, NIV). A mentality of division is not a mentality of peace. I am praying that we *all* adopt a mentality of thoughtful peace: peace that doesn't back down from the church that God has called us to create, and peace that understands the complications of a multicultural, reconciling church.

I am thankful that, as I tell my high school girls' small group, it is not my responsibility to change hearts and minds. I will continue to sow seeds on all ground: rocky, thorny, and hard-trodden path. Ultimately, it is the Spirit who will nourish those seeds. The church is complex, but at its head is Christ, more powerful and wise than any one member or governing body. If Christ can overcome death itself, surely he can overcome our human conflict.

I'd rather be excluded for who I include than included for who I exclude, but I don't want to exclude anyone. It seems that the structure of the church, tainted by human sin, has created a situation of an inevitable "us" and "them."

Even as everything seems broken, my experiences have shown me the difference between the structure of the church and the church.

The church is not the General Conference. The church is not The United Methodist Church. The church is not the Southern Baptist Church, the Episcopal Church, the Roman Catholic Church, or the Greek Orthodox Church.

Where two or more gather in Jesus' name, God is there. The church is praying with a friend before a meal, songs of love around a campfire, mucking out houses after a hurricane, giving immunizations to the uninsured.

We are broken, but Jesus wasn't crucified for flawless people. Our mission continues in our brokenness.

Lord, make us whole.
Let Your will be done here as in heaven.
Show us the way forward.

**Sydney Bertram** is a lifelong United Methodist and is currently a member of the Clemson (University) Wesley Foundation. She hopes to become a physician and work in the international missions field. When she's not studying, she enjoys hiking in the Southern Appalachians, running by the lake, and baking more desserts than she and her roommate can reasonably consume.

Clemson Class of '21

# CHAPTER THREE
# Sharon Bowers

Students Seek Safe Places:
Are We Providing Them?

**And different strokes for different folks**
**And so on and so on and scooby dooby doo**
**Oh sha sha we got to live together. I'm everyday people."[1]**

These are the lyrics taken from a Sly and the Family Stone's song "Everyday People" in the album *Stand* released in 1969. We could learn a valuable lesson from the lyrics in this song. That is, regardless of the General Conference 2019 ruling, as the people called Methodist, we have to find a way to live together despite our differences. If we continue speaking truth to power, we will find that we are much more alike than different. This is especially true in college and university campus ministries. It is on campus, in this privileged space, where students need and want discipleship and mentoring that is based on critical thinking, unconditional acceptance, love, and grace.

Many students are not afraid to advocate for the creation of safe places where they can learn and grow spiritually. It is on college campuses that students develop life long friendships, explore the tension between embedded and deliberative theology, practice spiritual disciplines, engage in spiritual formation, and learn to live out loud the principles of social justice and compassion through service learning. Because of the involvement in such life-shaping activities, students seek out safe places to live in, and beyond, the tensions.

Today's tough questions are considered in a totally different environment than in the past. The majority of twenty-first century college students do not remember a day without the use of the initialisms such as LGB, LGBT, or LGBTQIA+ to refer to members or allies of the gay community. Although these particular initial-

---

[1] Stone, Sly, "Everyday People," Stand, Epic Records, 1969.

isms have only been in mainstream society since the early 90's, the majority of college students on campuses have grown up fully aware of the terminology and what it and other terms frequently used in the gay community mean. These are labels used to self-iden-tify and describe many of their family and friends. So, it is no wonder that they are generally perplexed as they are faced with the daunting task of trying figure out what the "big deal" is anyway for so many other people. A world that is full of diversity and inclusion is a world full of "everyday people."

These students are routinely tasked with trying to wholly love the God that created them within the confines of an ever-evolving world where a mainstream heteronormative narrative says that it is impossible for them to do this when they or their friends are same-gender-loving. It is safe to say that although students arrive on campus with embedded theology and opinions, parental influ-ence regarding human sexuality does not sustained itself in the way other core beliefs and values have, such as racism, classism, and sexism. Not only are students hip on the various initialisms and descriptive language, they are more accepting, embracing, and empowering of individuals who identify as LGBTQIA+ than ever before. The stigma that has for many years left those who dared to "come out" bereft, has been replaced with signs of hope and solidar-ity that promotes inclusion and acceptance. Thus, yielding a sense of "okayness" with differences. Almost daily, a student sits across the desk from me and speaks in the affirmative regarding his or her sexuality. It is commonplace to hear students begin a conver-sation with the following: "As a gay male/female," "As a practicing lesbian," "As a transgender male/female, I ...." The sentence is usually completed with a statement of inquiry regarding how they can best live out their call to ministry in a world riddled with such religious complexities and exclusions.

The quest to find a place where one can "be who they be" is part of a never-ending journey for wholeness and wellness. In our day-to-day interaction, many students both gay and straight are seeking a safe place to learn and grow. Campus ministry provides this. We provide the space and place to explore the tensions that have been expanded by decisions such as those that came from General Confer-ence 2019. The mission at the University of Tennessee, Knoxville Wesley Foundation is to be an open, diverse Christian community, promoting spiritual growth, and extending God's love on campus. As we live out our faith, we are committed to **all** students. First, one of guiding principles is that **all** people are made in the image of God and therefore are worthy of respect and honor. Second, we are committed to engaging in three major areas of spiritual growth and formation as we engage the campus and the community in public discourse around race-ethnicity, human sexuality, and religion. We believe that exploring these possibilities will lend itself to making our campus, the community, and the world a better place. We are committed to heading toward a more inclusive church. As we find ourselves in the aftermath of the decisions of General Conference 2019, we solicit your prayers and invite you to join our campus ministry as people who would rather than stand bewildered on the banks of the shores of uncompromising traditions that fosters the ever-widening chasm between human sexuality and Christianity, jump in, and swim in the tensions. We are doing so by conversing, conferencing, and committing to a healthy discourse that brings about the necessary exchange. We are not afraid to sit in the tensions and wrestle with our theology so that which is embedded might become more deliberative.

> *"Today's tough questions are considered in a totally different environment than in the past. The majority of twenty-first century college students do not remember a day without the use of the initialisms such as LGBTQIA+."*

We are committed to providing programming and support for educational and spiritual leadership, resource development, and advocacy for compassion and justice ministries. We cannot afford to shy away from public discourse on religion and human sexuality. Human sexuality, Christianity, and gender identity are up close, personal, and in our face acting as agents of change, transforming our faith, and shaping the way we engage God and others. Our college and university campus ministries, albeit some under legal constraints, are committed to the full inclusion of all people regardless of race and ethnicity, gender and gender identity, culture, creed, and expression of sexual orientation. People deserve the opportunity to seek, learn, grow, and transform in a safe, non-threatening environment as they engage in spiritual formation. We do not judge or exclude people from joining our campus ministry (Wesley) or being part of our leadership team because of their sexual orientation or gender identity. The intersection of human sexuality, Christianity, and gender identity, along with the myriad of additional society confluences, must meet and mingle to foster an ideology where "open doors, open hearts, open people" is no longer seen as disingenuous.

We must continue our Methodist holy conferencing so that we

can listen to one another and continue to discern God's will for us both individually and collectively. It is critical that we promote an observable presence as we engage in the dismantling of institutional homophobia, racism, and sexism. We are the church and we must stay together creating "love nets" that when properly cast, catch "all" people and release none.

This is the Lord's Prayer for the *everyday people* called Methodist:

> [20]*"My prayer is not for them alone. I pray also for those who will believe in me through their message,* [21]*that all of them may be one, Father, just as you are in me and I am in you. May they also be in us so that the world may believe that you have sent me.* [22]*I have given them the glory that you gave me, that they may be one as we are one—* [23]*I in them and you in me—so that they may be brought to complete unity. Then the world will know that you sent me and have loved them even as you have loved me."*

**John 17:20-23, NIV**

**Dr. Sharon Bowers** is an elder in the Holston Conference of the The United Methodist Church. She serves as Executive Director of The University of Tennessee (Knoxville) Wesley Foundation. Prior to serving at the Wesley Foundation, she served appointments at Stanley UMC, Chattanooga, Tennessee and Randolph UMC, Pulaski, Virginia.

# CHAPTER FOUR

# Wil Cantrell
Existential Threats and a Pathway to Peace

As the debates raged at the 2019 General Conference of The United Methodist Church, I heard a common theme in the voices of conservative and progressive delegates and observers: desperation. Often taking the form of out-of-control emotions and devious legislative tactics, this desperation was on display from both sides. While it is easy to be offended by acts of desperation (especially when you are not the one feeling desperate), I found myself coming to recognize I might act similarly if I felt as desperate as others were feeling, and pondering where this desperation was coming from.

I believe the desperation we saw in many of the progressive protests and conservative rhetoric came from the same place: an existential threat. When faced with a threat to their identity or existence, people who otherwise respect and love one another can quickly resort to warfare. So, let's consider the source of these threats and then ask ourselves if there is any possible resolution available to us which protects all involved.

From the progressive side, the desperation came from feeling they were being expelled from a church they did not want to leave by legislation designed to place upon them requirements they could not possibly, in good conscience, meet. Pastors worried about losing their jobs. LGBTQIA+ persons felt like second-class citizens in the church that pledged to love, nurture, and support them at their baptisms. Parents mourned their children and grandchildren would no longer worship with them because our policies would cause them to feel unwelcome and unwanted. A whole group of people were losing their spiritual home, perhaps their most important home. And when your home is threatened, you'll do anything to defend it.

On the conservative side, delegates and observers often shared their fear that any degree of LGBTQIA+ inclusion would tear their churches apart from the inside out. In some instances, they feared such a change would destroy all The United Methodist churches in their region. In other cases, they feared allowing official recognition of differing opinions on Biblical interpretation regarding LGBTQIA+ inclusion would undercut the basic foundation for discerning truth upon which they based their religious beliefs and, in turn, create a slippery slope that might eventually lead to the basic tenets of the Christian faith being challenged. They, too, were fighting to protect their spiritual home.

The existence of these existential threats explains why each side fought so hard against the other and why no compromise could be reached. I initially understood the existential threat experienced by progressives, but I failed to fully understand the existential threat felt by conservatives. As the One Church Plan was debated, the existential threat felt by conservatives became more apparent to me. It was easy to me, as a moderate, to see the One Church Plan as a compromise. But it did not come across as a compromise to my conservative friends. It came across as an existential threat.

It has become clear to me that nothing like the One Church Plan or the "local option" will work for United Methodism. These solutions, while perhaps logical from an external perspective, simply provoke too many existential threats to those within the church.

What might work would be something new: something like the Connectional Conference Plan where we would almost entirely redo our denominational structure to make space for one another to follow our consciences where need be, and to allow us to be in ministry together wherever we can be.

At the recent General Conference, the Connectional Conference Plan was dismissed out of hand by many delegates (including myself) because the required two-thirds vote needed to pass its constitutional amendments seemed to be too unrealistic. So instead, we pitted the One Church Plan against the Traditional Plan and we bludgeoned one another with our words and attitudes. We left General Conference with a conservative legislative victory which might not be able to be enforced and untold collateral damage (in the form of those who have become disillusioned about the Christian faith and The United Methodist Church thanks to our behavior) which we all mourn.

Now that we know the One Church Plan or local option will not work whatsoever and if it proves that the passage of the Traditional Plan ends up being merely an extension of the status quo because of the inability to enforce its provisions, then it may be that a groundswell of momentum will emerge for a vast restructuring which provides enough space to protect the consciences of all sides and enough unity to magnify our witness for Christ throughout the world.

Many people predicted that whichever side lost the vote at

General Conference would leave the UMC in mass in the weeks which followed. So far this has not occurred. Instead, people of varying perspectives have reaffirmed their love of Christ, their love for one another, and their love of the UMC.

In the time since General Conference, many private conversations have been taking place among bishops, moderate and progressive leaders, and conservative leaders. This is a good thing. We legislated our way into this situation. We will not legislate our way out of it. What must take place prior to the 2020 General Conference are organic expressions of holy conferencing where leaders within our denomination can listen to the voices of their constituents and of other leaders on the other side of the issue to discern if there can be a way forward which does not existentially threaten progressive or conservatives.

No one was surprised in 1968 at the Uniting Conference when the merger between the Evangelical United Brethren and the Methodist Church was approved, creating The United Methodist Church, because all the difficult debates had been hashed out well ahead of time. Any way forward for the UMC which maintains substantive unity among its major constituencies will be achieved in a similar manner. While prior to the 2019 General Conference, I thought the two-third vote required for constitutional amendments was too high a bar for any legislation to climb over, I now believe any legislation designed to offer a Way Forward, which cannot achieve a two-thirds vote, is a way apart rather than a way forward.

Trust is so low and animosity is so high between the two sides who have desperately fought against one another for years now, however, it could be that no grand compromise of this sort can take place in the near future. Instead, what might happen is that either progressive and moderates leave if the environment becomes too hostile, or conservatives leave if they grow too weary of the fight to enforce the Traditional Plan. In this case, we might see new expressions of Methodism split off from United Methodism and then after splitting off, these branches of Methodism may find ways to connect again to one another in order to share in the 99% of our mission and ministry that we all agree upon. In this way, an arrangement like the Connectional Conference Plan could develop over time organically.

Of course, I have no crystal ball to help me see the future. I do know this: God is our redeemer. Our God wastes nothing. God will redeem the devastation and harm caused by five decades of in-fighting to help birth new expressions of vibrant Methodist Christianity which we have not yet imagined.

Eight days after the 2019 General Conference concluded, United Methodists around the world gathered in their churches to have the symbol of the cross placed on their foreheads with ashes as a reminder that when we die to ourselves, we find "the life that is truly life" in Jesus Christ (1 Timothy 6:19, NIV).

As I was administering the ashes at my local church this year, a six-year-old girl came forward with her mother to receive the ashes. Now, to say this little girl looked cute as button would be to vastly overestimate the cuteness of buttons. She was much cuter than any button I have ever seen. She had picked out a nice dress for the occasion, curled her hair, and she smiled at me with a sweetness and kindness which defied words. I smiled back and bent down to put the ashes on her forehead, but when I began to speak, the words would not come out. I choked up and tears filled my eyes. How could I say to this little girl she was going to die one day?

I took a deep breath and tried again. No luck. I considered just telling her that Jesus loves her. Yet, I had this suspicion that doing so would short-change the message. So, with all the strength I could muster, I managed to say, "You are dust and to dust you will return. Repent and believe the Gospel." She just kept smiling at me. Apparently, she could handle the truth better than I could.

It is hard to acknowledge that the things which have brought the most beauty to our lives cannot stay the way the way we remember them or the way they are right now. I pray, however, the greatest beauty in that young lady's life will not be the ribbons and curls of her childhood, but the sacrificial love she exudes throughout her life as she learns what it means to die and rise with Christ. And I pray the greatest beauty of The United Methodist witness, will not be its infancy in the 1960s, but will be the ongoing way United Methodists learn to make room for the Holy Spirit to work by making room for one another on all sides of the globe and on all sides of our current disagreements regarding our Social Principles.

Out of the ashes come life. That's how it's always been. And I believe that's how it will be when we look back upon the ultimate work God performs among us, and in spite of us, in this time of struggle.

God's blessing to you all! I feel blessed beyond measure to be one of the people called Methodist and to share a church with people like you.

**Wil Cantrell** serves as Senior Associate Pastor of Concord United Methodist Church in Farragut, TN. Wil was elected to serve on the General and Jurisdictional Conference delegations from the Holston Conference in 2012 & 2016/19 and 2001-2005 Executive Committee of the World Methodist Council.

He is the author of the recently released book *Unafraid and Unashamed: Facing the Future of the United Methodism* (Market Square Books).

# CHAPTER FIVE
# Bishop Kenneth L. Carder
The Way Forward: Repentance and Confession

Pivotal events in history are always more complicated than meets the eye and it takes time and distance to fully understand and learn their lessons. The called session of the General Conference is one of those pivotal episodes in United Methodist history which merits ongoing analyses by church historians, theologians, and other leaders. Historians for years to come will sift through the rubble of a collapsed, or at least diminished, institutional church for clues as to the contributing factors.

Admittedly, my perspectives on the questions "Where are we as a denomination?" and "Where do we go from here?" are limited and perhaps premature. However, having spent more than a half century in leadership positions within The United Methodist Church as pastor, bishop, and seminary professor, I have participated in assumptions, decisions, and practices that contributed to the debacle in St. Louis.

Therefore, my reflections are more confessional than prescriptive. The called session of General Conference exposed deep and long-standing idolatries and failures within United Methodism. The debacle in St. Louis saw the "chickens come home to roost" or the reaping of a harvest of seeds sown as early as the formation of the Methodist Episcopal Church in 1784.

Whatever organizational directions result from the present conflicts and confusion, there are theological and polity issues that merit attention. Learning the lessons from the past and discerning a new future will require continuing conversation grounded in our theological foundations, a common vision of God's reign brought near in Jesus Christ, and humility before the Triune God who is forever making all things new.

What follows are some of my convictions forged in my own struggle over more than five decades of participation in the ministry of the denomination that has shaped my life. I'm uncertain as to the structural changes implied in the convictions or the specific next steps. Since our current situation developed over at least two centuries, the needed changes will require decades of faithful struggle to read the signs of the times in the light of God's present and coming reign of compassion, justice, generosity, and peace.

**Confession One: The first step forward is repentance, an honest facing of the idolatries, brokenness, and sins that have brought us to where we are as a denomination and turning toward a new future.**

Repentance is always the genesis of new birth and transformation. It is the initial and ongoing invitation of Jesus. His public ministry began with a summons toward a new future: "Now, after John was arrested, Jesus came to Galilee, proclaiming the good news of God, and saying, 'The time is fulfilled, and the kingdom of God has come near; repent and believe in the good news'" (Mark 1:14 NRSV).

There can be no faithful move forward without consciously and intentionally examining currently misplaced loyalties and priorities. Without such candid, ongoing, and painful self-examination, we will build new structures and practices on fatally flawed foundations where the termites continue their destruction. Without repentance, the organizational and programmatic changes made will be but improved means to unimproved ends.

Since the General Conference in February, lament over the impasse and the harm being inflicted on one another has characterized much of the conversation. That is a positive sign! Lament is akin to repentance. Authentic lament, however, involves a turning away from the destructive practices causing the suffering and destructiveness and turning toward practices that reconcile and transform.

Repentance is hard, persistent work and cannot be limited to an hour-long worship service or a liturgical prayer of confession. Rather, repentance is a way of being, an orientation of humble self-awareness and a constant openness to the guidance of the Holy Spirit present within community. It involves naming the sins, idolatries, and misguided choices that fall short of God's intentions as individuals and as the church.

Engaging in what one church historian calls "expansion by

24

evasion"[1] is one of our denominational sins which contributes to our current crisis. The malignant cancer of institutional triumphalism has existed as far back as the beginning of the Methodist Episcopal Church. The most striking expression was the compromise on slavery at General Conferences following the Christmas Conference of 1784, which adopted John Wesley's strong position against slavery.

Methodism grew rapidly on the American frontier and became addicted to bigness and institutional prominence. Methodism easily acclimated to the American values of individualism and the market logic of exchange and expansion. Church growth was part of our over-arching goal long before it became a programmatic strategy.

For fear of losing the support of slaveholders and sympathizers in the South, subsequent conferences softened the antislavery stance. Many argued that "winning souls" was the church's mission, not engaging in the politics of slavery, and "winning souls" translated into increasing membership. A result was the bifurcation of the gospel and reducing holiness to personal piety without social righteousness.

The split in 1844 creating the Methodist Episcopal Church and the Methodist Episcopal Church, South, did result in maintaining and even increasing the total membership of the two denominations. The cost to Methodism's moral authority and theological integrity, however, was incalculable.

American church historian, Clarence C. Goen, chronicles the failure of mainline denominations to provide leadership on the critical issue of slavery and thereby becoming complicit in the violence of the 1860s and beyond. He suggests that the first phase of dealing with conflicts is moral persuasion through teaching, proclamation, and dialogue. When that fails, legislation ensues with penalties for disobedience. When legislation fails, violence becomes the accepted response.

The United Methodist Church is again at a critical juncture when it comes to moral authority, theological integrity, and faithful witness. Instead of repentance for our history of elevating institutional expansion and dominance above faithfulness to God's reign of justice, compassion, generosity, and hospitality, the focus is once

---

[1] Goen, C.C., *Broken Churches, Broken Nation: Denominational Schism and the Coming of the American Civil War* (Macon, Ga.: Mercer University Press, 1986), 147. Dr. Goen's book should be read by every United Methodist leader, especially the chapter entitled "A Failure of Leadership." He affirms throughout the book that the schism in mainline churches in the 1840s was the precursor to the Civil War, and the failure of the churches to theologically and ethically confront the injustice of slavery among their own members contributed to the violence of the Civil War.

again on perpetuating the practice of "expansion by evasion" and multiplying by dividing.

**Confession Two: Schism within the body of Christ represents failure, as divorce is emblematic of a failed marriage.**

Sometimes divorce is the preferred way forward given irreconcilable differences and debilitating conflicts within a marriage. Nevertheless, divorce is not the goal of any marriage. It is a compromise of the couple's best intentions. Failure to acknowledge and deal with the underlying dynamics resulting in the divorce will almost certainly perpetuate those dynamics in future relationships.

Division within The United Methodist Church may be a way of interrupting the cycle of harm, but it falls short of God's intentional will for the oneness and wholeness of Christ's body. The refusal to acknowledge the antecedents to the current talk of possible schism will only perpetuate the dysfunction. Future controversial and challenging issues will most certainly emerge, resulting in conflict and calls for additional structural splits unless we pause to repent and begin to turn in new directions.

We share a long history of denominational divorces without authentic repentance and bringing forth fruit worthy of repentance. Methodism as a denomination began in a split from the Church of England, which had separated from Roman Catholicism, which experienced its own schism with the Protestant Reformation. Division has characterized Protestantism from the beginning and has proliferated into more than twelve hundred denominations in the United States alone.

Not only have we not repented for our corporate failure to reflect the unity integral to the very nature of the Triune God, we have adopted schism as a strategy for church growth and called it evangelism. A leader of the Wesley Covenant Association recently reflected the dangerous notion of schism as an appropriate strategy for church growth:

> Given the dramatic decline in worship attendance, the proposed drastic budget cuts, and a bitter debate that has deepened the discord in the church, perhaps now is the time to seriously consider separation as the most God honoring way forward.[2]

---

[2] Fenton, Walter, "Proposed Budget Cuts Add to UM Church's Challenges," April 9, 2019, Wesleyan Covenant Association, https://wesleyancovenant.org/2019/04/08/proposed-budget-cuts-add-to-um-churchs-challenges/.

Call separation a compromise within the current context, but let's not call it "the most God honoring way forward." Clothing schism in pious garments of honoring God is akin to dressing Jesus in kingly attire while crucifying him. God is honored when the church reflects the unity within and among the Father, Son, and Holy Spirit. At least, let us acknowledge honestly and repentantly that "we have sinned and fall short of the glory of God" (Romans 3:23, NIV) in our inability to deal with conflicts in the way the Triune God deals with us.

> *"The inability to redemptively address differences on such issues as human sexuality and interpretation of Scripture reveals underlying malignant hubris."*

Multiplication by division operates naturally in the biological world and it may produce temporary growth in the ecclesial world. But the fastest growing cells in the human body tend to be cancerous cells! Healing requires interrupting the growth of malignant cells and nurturing healthy ones. Cultivating malignant cells hastens death!

The inability to redemptively address differences on such issues as human sexuality and interpretation of Scripture reveals underlying malignant hubris. Such pride elevates certainty above faith, rigidity above mystery, law above grace, haughtiness above holiness, coercion above persuasion, and exclusion above welcoming.

John Wesley acknowledged that schism is a failure to love.[3] At the core of Wesleyan theology and practice are these phrases: holiness of heart and life, the entire love of God shed abroad in human hearts, perfection in love, love for God and neighbor, watch over one another in love. Class meetings, bands, and societies were instituted as means of forming people in love. For Wesley, the primary role of doctrine is formational, not juridical or informational. The test of faithfulness to Christian doctrine is the character of those who claim allegiance to the doctrine, and the model or image of character is love as Christ loves.

The embarrassing acrimony on public display in St. Louis at the General Conference was the culmination of our failure to form one another in agape, the love poured out in Jesus Christ. In the name of defending biblical truth and doctrinal orthodoxy, we failed the core test of Christian discipleship—LOVE! Agape/Love is more than

---

[3] See John Wesley's sermons, "On Schism," "Caution Against Bigotry," and "Catholic Spirit."

emotional sentiment, or warm feelings, or uniformity of belief, or abstract theory. The love of which Jesus is the embodiment includes acceptance of and respect for the other, *every* other, as a beloved child of God made in the divine image with infinite worth and dignity, whose gifts and uniqueness are celebrated and welcomed as means of grace for the common good. It is holding one another in compassion and solidarity as we all grow toward perfection in love.

Separating Christian disciples according to secularly derived labels such as "traditionalists," "progressives," "conservatives," and "liberals" mocks the Apostle Paul's God-inspired declaration: "There is no longer Jew or Greek, there is no longer slave or free, there is no longer male or female; for all of you are one in Christ Jesus" (Galatians 3:28, NRSV). Schism is failure to live the reconciliation and unity already effected in the life, teaching, death, and resurrection of Jesus the Christ!

**Confession Three: Renewal is the work of the Holy Spirit and in the Triune God's time and through God's own surprising instruments.**

I've lived through many "renewal" strategies designed to bring new life to The Methodist Church. The statistical decline of the Methodists in America began during my early years as a pastor, the 1950s and 1960s. A church strategist said at the time that the Sunday school was the key to the church's future and if the decline in attendance was not reversed, the denomination would die. "As the Sunday school goes, so goes the church," I heard him say.

Strategies were developed by what was then the Board of Education. New interactive educational resources were developed, introduced, and implemented across the denomination. It was a massive church-wide effort. One of the components was training teachers in the new curriculum and visiting in each Methodist home to introduce the curriculum. We followed the plan in my local church and experienced an upturn in attendance. What made the difference, however, was the visitation in the homes, not the curriculum itself. The bump in attendance was short-lived!

Throughout the intervening years, multiple initiatives and strategies have emerged with promises of denominational revitalization. Some have focused on organizational structures, others on programmatic emphases. Some originated with General Conference and annual conferences, while others were in the form of episcopal initiatives or general agency programming. The efforts have been well-intentioned, and many resulted in improvements and at least temporary and localized revitalization.

A more recent initiative in which I was personally and strongly invested was the Episcopal Initiative on Children and Poverty. The Initiative's goal was stated as follows: "The renewal of the church in response to the God who is among the least of these." The bishops unanimously approved the Initiative and spent time over two quadrennia in pursuing the goals with mixed results. The Initiative was on the agenda of the Oxford Institute of Methodist Theological Studies in 1997 and I was asked to provide an overview to Methodist scholars and other leaders from across the globe. Following the presentation and at the invitation of my friend Douglas Meeks, I had dinner with Jurgen Moltman.

In response to my request for input, the famed theologian remarked, "The power of the initiative is its theology, the focus on joining God's presence among the weak and vulnerable. Don't let it become an appeal to general humanitarianism. If it loses focus on God, it will become another programmatic effort with little power and diminishing participation."

His warning was prophetic! While the Initiative had some success in raising awareness and birthing important ministries, the overarching goal of "renewal in response to the God who is among the least of these" remains unachieved. The Council of Bishops set it aside in 2004 and subsequently included it under four programmatic foci as "ministry with the poor." The Council's focus turned to responding to membership decline by attentiveness to "making disciples of Jesus Christ for the transformation of the world." That effort soon developed into the "Call to Action" which sought renewal through structural changes. Those changes were soundly rebuffed by the General Conference of 2012.

I expressed to a theologian friend my discouragement over the Council of Bishops pushing aside the Initiative on Children and Poverty. The theological consultant with the Initiative remarked, "We had hoped that the Initiative would facilitate renewal, but renewal is not within our power. It is the work of the Holy Spirit in God's time!" Another theologian stated it starkly, "The United Methodist Church is atheist! It doesn't need God! It presumes that renewal will come from a 'strategic plan' and a clever marketing effort. The God of Jesus has a way of upsetting our strategic plans and slick marketing. The cross never fits into our institutional preservation efforts!" He added, "The church should only do those things that rely on God to accomplish."

Only the Triune God can repair the brokenness of The United

Methodist Church and bring renewal. It will not come through legislation, judicial processes, organizational tinkering, or public relation strategies. Those are, at best, bandages and soothing ointments applied to gaping wounds and cancerous sores, unless they emerge from deep encounter with the God who is in solidarity with those Jesus called "the least of these" and Charles Wesley referred to as "Jesus' bosom friends," the vulnerable and oppressed.

Renewal seldom comes at the hands of the institutionally powerful and privileged. God's knack for choosing the least and the outsiders is well documented: an aged Abraham and Sarah, a murderer-on-the-run Moses, an exiled remnant captive in Babylon, a pagan Cyrus, a peasant teenage maiden Mary, a middle eastern terrorist Saul. But the supreme means of the renewal of human hearts, communities, institutions, and the entire cosmos is One born among the homeless, in infancy lived as an immigrant, grew up in a remote village among the working class, was executed as a convicted felon, and buried in a borrowed tomb.

Therein is the revelation of the way toward renewal. It lies in identification with the poor, the oppressed, the excluded, the pushed aside, the abused, the powerless, the scorned. There is where God is most clearly, radically, redemptively, and transformatively present! Who are the pushed aside, excluded, abused, and scorned in today's United Methodist Church?

Included in that company of God's beloved children are LGBTQIA+ people and their families. Rather than being threats to the church's renewal, they may quite possibly be the means by which God is seeking to bring wholeness and renewal to the very institution that seeks to exclude them from full participation. Solidarity with them in the pursuit of God's present and coming reign brought near in Jesus Christ and receiving their gifts may very well release anew the power of God's all-inclusive and all-transforming grace.

**Confession Four: God's reign of compassion, justice, generosity, hospitality, and peace will prevail, with or without The United Methodist Church's existence.**

Jesus' primary invitation was and is to join him in living toward a new world dawning in him. He called it the "kingdom of God" or some prefer the term "kin-dom." The final loyalty is to God's reign or what Paul called "the new creation" and the Book of Revelation refers to as "a new heaven and new earth."

One of the idolatries for which repentance is needed remains our substitution of the penultimate, the church, for the ultimate, the new creation shaped by God's reign. God's preoccupation is far more universal and cosmic than the institutional prominence or even survival of The United Methodist Church. It is nothing less than the reconciliation of the entire cosmos to its original intent, an expression of the very nature and love of God, the Creator!

Among the components of God's reign are these:

- All creation healed from the scarred majestic mountains to the polluted flowing streams, from the microscopic diseased cell to the threated ozone

- All people know their identity as precious sons and daughters whose worth and dignity do not lie in their capacities, or physical features, or social prestige, or sexual orientation, but in the one to whom they belong

- All barriers of race, class, ethnicity, nationality, political or religious affiliation, sexual identity, or social status are removed and the human family lives as one under the parenthood of a loving God

- All people have access to that which is necessary for flourishing as beloved children of God and "justice roll(s) down like waters and righteousness like a never-failing stream" (Amos 5:24, NIV)

- All nations and communities live in peace as "the wolf shall live with the lamb, the leopard shall lie down with the kid, the calf and the lion and fatling together, and a little child shall lead them" (Isaiah 11:6, NIV).

The church exists to be a herald, sign, foretaste, and instrument of God's vision for ALL creation. How closely the institutional church and our congregations resemble that vision is the criteria we should use to evaluate faithfulness and renewal. A church with a vision no larger than institutional survival and denominational dominance will not and has no reason to survive! Only a church shaped by God's love for ALL has a future!

The good news is this: God's new creation will come to completion! The decisive victory has already been won in the birth, life, teachings, death, and resurrection of Jesus the Christ. Therein lies our hope in these turbulent times for "the people called Methodist."

## Conclusion

There is widespread agreement that The United Methodist Church is in crisis. The institution's future is in jeopardy. The called session of General Conference in St. Louis, February 2019, will be marked as a turning point by future historians. One thing is for certain: It is time for serious, intentional, and soul-searching evaluation. It is an occasion for repentance, a turning away from idolatries, misplaced priorities, and misguided practices AND a turning toward a new future that has already been made known and brought near in Jesus the Christ.

We can repent without defensiveness and move forward with courage and hope because Easter has come! God has won and God will win! Therefore, we can live now in the light of God's present and coming triumph. The institution known as The United Methodist Church may not survive! But the future of the Body of Christ is not in jeopardy! It has already been raised from the dead. The Risen One goes before us! The invitation is to follow him where he goes, love and welcome those whom he loves and for whom he died, and join him in the hurting and broken places of the world.

"The time is fulfilled, and the kingdom of God has come near; repent, and believe the good news" (Mark 1:14 NRSV).

**Bishop Kenneth L. Carder** retired as an active bishop in 2004 after serving the Nashville Area (1992-2000) and the Mississippi Area (2004). Prior to his election to the episcopacy, he served local churches in the Holston Conference, including Concord in Farragut, TN, First Church Oak Ridge, and Church Street in Knoxville. As an active bishop he authored the Foundation Document for the Initiative on Children and Poverty, chaired the committee that developed "A Wesleyan Vision for Theological Education and Leadership for the 21st Century," and delivered the Episcopal Address at the 2004 General Conference. Bishop Carder joined the faculty of Duke Divinity School in 2004 and was subsequently named Ruth W. and A. Morris Williams Distinguished Professor and is now Distinguished Professor Emeritus.

He currently serves as volunteer chaplain of a memory care facility and as caregiver for his wife, Linda. He is the author of six books including *Ministry with the Forgotten: Dementia through a Spiritual Lens* to be released by Abingdon Press in September 2019.

# CHAPTER SIX
# Bishop Ken Carter
To Redefine our Present Connectionality:
Thoughts on a Way Beyond the Way Forward

## A Personal Word

I was attracted to contribute to this collection of essays because of the diversity of perspectives. I want to tell you about my perspective, and to speak directly to those who might differ.

As I write, I serve as the president of the Council of Bishops of our global church and residential bishop of Florida, a large and diverse annual conference. I served previously as one of three moderators of the Commission on a Way Forward.

I supported the One Church Plan, as did the great majority of the Council of Bishops. My endorsement of this plan was based on three factors: it honored our very different contexts, it allowed for freedom of conscience at the local level, and it removed the "incompatibility" language.

In my mind, the One Church Plan did not ask anyone to depart. I do understand that it was unacceptable to many among our most conservative and progressive members. It did not fully honor their convictions.

At the same time, I worked to assure fairness in the process. All three plans were included in the final reports (written and verbal) to the Special Session. All three plans were presented to the Judicial Council for constitutional review. I have sat at the table with United Methodists across the world who envision a very different future for our denomination.

All of this is to say that I seek to speak to the whole church. I am a person with a very traditional faith who imagines a church that removes obstacles to inclusion and acceptance of all people. And my belief in the power of the Triune God leads me to believe that this can be our shared future.

My hopeful nature motivates me to work for this. My realistic nature understands that this is not a given. The Special Session has sharpened our differences.

So where do we go next?

## Listening Across Differences

In my sermon at the beginning of the Special Session of the General Conference, I made reference to an extraordinary *Ted Talk* by the Nigerian author Chimamanda Adichie entitled "The Danger of a Single Story." It has been viewed by seventeen million people.

The simple, and yet profound, thesis in her talk is that we have different stories. We need to share them, and we also need to honor the differences, and recognize the harm in imagining that ours is the only story.

In the weeks after St. Louis, there is not one response, but many. I note a few:

- **Harm**—The testimony of many LGBTQIA+ persons and their allies that the words of our church have done and continue to do harm to them and to those on the periphery of our church who feel excluded from God's welcome.

- **Conscience**—The struggles of many of our members about how to remain in a church that is identified with our present language about homosexuality.

- **Fatigue**—The sense of many conservatives and progressives that this is a recurring experience which in their minds is an unnecessary expenditure of time, energy, and resources.

- **Anxiety**—The experience of some leaders in central conferences who see this as a primarily U.S. and Western European matter, and whose concern is about disruption of mission partnerships.

- **Differentiation**—The strategy of many local churches that are re-branding themselves with a counter-narrative to the General Conference, through either banners or full-page newspaper ads or sermons.

- **Resistance**—The actions of many that are in direct contrast to the polity of the church, for the purpose of social change, and the responses of those who monitor them.

- **Reorientation**—The hope of many that the church will now give its attention to other matters of concern, among them poverty, local church vitality, climate change, and racism.

These are some, but not all of our stories. We are clearly in a place of struggle, as a 55-45 or 53-47 church. There are strong opinions and passions embedded in these differing stories.

## Searching for a Core

My continuing question has been about a sufficiently common narrative to keep us in communion with each other, a narrative that would be the fulfillment of the epiclesis, that the Holy Spirit would *"make us one with Christ, one with each other and one in ministry to all the world."*

For me, there is the clear New Testament teaching about unity, which is also at the heart of my calling as a bishop. I refer to passages like John 17, I Corinthians 12-14, and Ephesians 4, and my consecration promise to seek the unity of the church.

But underneath this call for unity are very real differences, and a question: Are our differences so profound that they prohibit us from being in communion or connection with each other?

A great deal of work has been, and is being, done to achieve some kind of division or separation or space between us. I take these conversations to be the work of faithful people. And yet I remain called and encouraged by many to more clearly name what we do have in common. Or, to say it differently, if we were to begin again and construct a church from the ground up, what would be the essentials, or the core, of our life together?

My list of core practices - and our heritage is one of practical divinity - would look something like this:

- The Scriptures

- Apostles' and Nicene Creeds

- The Articles of Religion and the Confession of Faith

- Wesley's view of Prevenient, Justifying, and Sanctifying Grace

- The General Rules

- The Wesley Hymns (for example, "And Can It Be," "A Charge to Keep," "O For A Thousand Tongues to Sing," and "Love Divine, All Loves Excelling")

- Small Group Accountability and Support (Class and Band Meetings)

- Services of Baptism and Eucharist

- Works of Piety, Mercy, and Justice

- Recognition of Orders of Clergy across differently defined expressions of Methodism

- A shared Methodist/Wesleyan history, even with our divisions and yes, our failures/sins that call for repentance

- Shared Mission Work

- Shared Services

- A connectional way of life that includes forms of 1) superintendency for the purpose of accountability to the mission, 2) itineracy for the purpose of multiplication, and 3) conferencing for the purpose of inspiration, support, and governance

- An assumption that theology has practical (moral) implications and that the law is fulfilled through love

- A desire to share our faith in healthy and positive ways

- A desire to experience the Holy Spirit in our lives

- A posture of "convicted humility."

We are in a season of ambiguity and chaos; some of this is the reality of a global and democratic church, and some is a factor of profoundly different readings of what happened in St. Louis. Is this a problem? Or instead, is there a danger in a single story?

The adaptive work in this season might be to simply live our way into a new form of church, which was and remains within the Mission, Vision, and Scope of the Way Forward. If we are to truly move beyond the present impasse, a mature practice of the faith that honors our differences and that is truly open to the narratives of each other will be essential.

## Hungering for Justice and Reconciliation

We grieve the harm done to LGBTQIA+ persons. The Council of Bishops expressed this also in a pastoral letter in December, 2018. This has been my own language to the LGBTQIA+ community:

> *You are of sacred worth. You are not the problem. You are not out there. You have been in every church I have ever served. You have blessed me and our family. Your gifts strengthen the church. And my calling, for you and all people, is to remove the obstacles to your experience of the grace of God, and especially in the life of The United Methodist Church.*

The continuing work of justice in relation to the Special Session of the General Conference is in the hands of the General Commission of the General Conference (the executive committee of the Council of Bishops asked for an independent investigation into potential voting irregularities) and the Judicial Council's determination of the constitutionality of the actions of the General Conference.

I see hope in the conversations that are happening across the church. Gil Rendle has noted that conversation is the currency of change. Some conversation is between centrists and progressives. Some conversation is between conservatives leaning in and conservatives leaning out. Some conversations are for the purpose of unity. Some conversations are for the purpose of division. More conversation is better than less conversation.

When persons are harmed, the responses are understandable. Some want to create distance. Some shut down. And some retaliate.

I continue to affirm, perhaps especially now, the resources contained in *The Anatomy of Peace* and the work the Commission on a Way Forward did on convicted humility. In the season of Lent following the Special Session I began to read Thomas a Kempis' *The Imitation of Christ*. I was struck by the centrality of humility in that spiritual classic.

I also continue to reflect on 2 Corinthians 5, and Paul's vision for reconciliation. The Greek word for reconciliation is *katallage*. It is a word that appears only three times in the New Testament, and was a word more commonly used in politics than in religion. It is a word about settling disputes.

God settled a despite with us through the cross. This came through his humility and kenosis (Philippians 2). And God now asks us to move toward, not away from each other, as we take up this ministry of reconciliation. It is linked, Paul will go on to say in the first verses of 2 Corinthians 6, to our salvation. Our salvation is not in fleeing from each other. The Triune God did not flee from us. Our salvation is the way of the cross, our settling disputes with each other.

Our hope is in the power and providence of God, in whose image we are all created, in whose church we joined through public promises, and into whose agenda we are invited.

That agenda is to resist the forces of evil, injustice, and oppression, and to turn to the crucified and risen Jesus, our judge and our hope. This will be the imitation of Christ.

## Avoiding Harm in our Reading of Scripture

In my role as bishop, I receive a steady stream of letters. The great majority of them express two distinct values, and they can be summarized as follows:

- I want the church to love all people.

- I want the church to teach the Word of God.

If you have read this far, we are in some kind of relationship. And so, I owe it to you to be honest about my hopes and dreams for the church.

- I want the church to love all people.

- And I learned this from reading the Word of God.

I have no desire to distinguish between a church that loves all people and a love for the Word of God.

If you want to quote Leviticus, I can place that verse in the context of Jesus' Sermon on the Mount. If you want to quote Romans 1, I can place that verse in the context of Romans 2 and 3.

If you want to quote Jesus' teaching about marriage, we can place that in a broader context of what he was saying about divorce.

With eloquence, we can quote scripture to each other. Of course, I could do this without love. And where I have not done this, forgive me. Paul warns me about this in 1 Corinthians 13. If I understand all mysteries, but do not have love, I gain nothing.

I have given my life to studying, teaching, and preaching the Word of God. Do I understand it perfectly? I do not.

God has more to teach me, and this is the work of the Holy Spirit (John 16).

As a pastor, I have tried to love the people God has placed under my watch. A bishop is a shepherd. Do I offer the love of God to all people? In the words of the hymn, "Do I empty myself of all but love?" I do not. This is the ongoing process of sanctification.

Yes, we are deeply divided. We have done harm to each other. Some of us are passionate about loving all people. Some of us are passionate about the Word of God.

> **"I'm not smoothing over anything. This is a hard place."**

Will the church divide along these lines? It is an absurd possibility. Must the church cast out one of these voices? It is a definite strategy.

I'm not smoothing over anything. This is a hard place. People have been shaped and formed and they (we) will resist change. Change comes, in my experience, when we look into the face of a child, grandchild, or friend who is going through a divorce, a struggle with gender identity, an addiction, or an imprisonment.

We begin to hope that justice is restorative, that grace is amazing, that love bears all things, believes all things, hopes all things, endures all things (1 Corinthians 13). We search for a doctrine that sounds more like our favorite hymn or praise song than a set of rules.

We know about change in our spiritual and theological tradition. We even know the Greek word for change (*metanoia*). And, as one of my favorite Bible professors at Duke Divinity School, Mickey Efird would say, "That and fifty cents would get me a cup of coffee in hell!"

Change comes when we repent. The problem with this is that we want the other person to repent!

But, along the way, we do change.

When this happens, we begin to reframe the Word of God. Or, the Word becomes flesh, and this teaches us something about what we bring to reading the Word of God. We bring, at our best, a convicted humility. Wesley's Catholic Spirit was the ancestor of convicted humility. "Convicted humility" was a term articulated by the Commission on a Way Forward in service to the Special Session, and is defined as follows:

> *We begin from the recognition that our members hold a wide range of positions regarding same-sex relations and operate out of sincerely held beliefs. They are convinced of the moral views they espouse, and seek to be faithful to what they see as the truth God calls the church to uphold. It remains the case that their views on this matter are distinctly different, and in some cases cannot*

*be reconciled. We pray the exaggeration of our differences will not divide us. We also recognize and affirm that as United Methodists we hold in common many more fundamental theological commitments, commitments which bind us together despite our real differences. These also have implications for how we understand and express our disagreements, and for what we do about them.*

*Therefore, we seek to advocate a stance we have called convicted humility. This is an attitude which combines honesty about the differing convictions which divide us with humility about the way in which each of our views may stand in need of corrections. It also involves humble repentance for all the ways in which we have spoken and acted as those seeking to win a fight rather than those called to discern the shape of faithfulness together. In that spirit, we wish to lift up the shared core commitments which define the Wesleyan movement, and ground our search for wisdom and holiness.*

*We remain persuaded that the fruitfulness of the church and its witness to a fractured world are enhanced by our willingness to remain in relationship with those who share our fundamental commitments to scripture and our doctrinal standards, and yet whose views of faithfulness in this regard differ from our own.*

**Daily Christian Advocate, p.127**

A shared future is possible if we can engage in two spiritual practices:

- Refuse to see love for all people and the teaching of the Word of God as two separate things.

- Practice Convicted Humility.

## Designing the Next Church

If The United Methodist Church were to dissolve, if a group prevails with "enforcement mechanisms" that would clearly drive away significant sectors of the church, or if a conservative wing of the church were to depart, what could be lost?

Suppose, a magazine is published for decades. Its primary purpose is a focus on what is wrong with The United Methodist Church, every month. Many of us could spend a day filling newsprint with all that is wrong with the church. And many have spent a lifetime deconstructing the church. Each can be a lucrative calling.

It tells one part of the story.

It does not tell another part of the story. That is what is right with the church, and what could be lost.

**So, what could be lost?**

- **Relationships among people who love each other.** People who sing in choirs together, who have gone on mission trips together, who have studied the Bible together. People who have gone to seminary together, who have ministered together. People who have led us to Christ. People who have walked our spiritual journey. People who have mentored us.

  I am convinced that the group that wants to divide or dissolve the church or send a part of the church away is not the majority. It does have an amplified voice.

- **Mission from the local to the global level.** How we respond to life and death human needs will simply become collateral damage should we dissolve, divide, or send a part of the church away. Resources will be diverted. Systems of mission and justice will be dismantled, and they will end. Relationships will turn inward, through the grief and harm we have experienced.

  I am convinced that our unity is not based on our agreements. Our unity is based on our mission. What is this mission? To make disciples. To repair the world.

- **Opportunities for the next generation.** With the dissolution, division, or sending away of a part of the church, we have also cared for the retirement of clergy. Thank God. And most of the actors in this drama are of retirement age or approaching this season. But what about young adults preparing for ministry or the mission field, students in seminaries, or young adults in ministry? Again, these are simply not questions that are cared for in many of the conversations related to life beyond a Way Forward.

  I am convinced that young adults are not ideological about the relation of unity and LGBTQIA+ identity. Should we dissolve, divide, or send a part of the church away, the next generations will reconnect us. This has happened before.

41

The question, "What could be lost?" is relevant in conversations about departure, division, a new denomination, or the status quo.

Yet, loss is both the present reality and the inevitable next chapter. How do we find a way forward, post-St. Louis?

## Reclaim the Mission, Vision, and Scope of a Way Forward

Our work would be healthier if we saw ourselves in continuity with the Commission on a Way Forward and the bishops. Still, the realism that is needed is the lack of response of the Special Session to this prior work, especially the mission, vision, and scope (MVS), and the theological statement, with the recognition that something profoundly new is taking shape.

Our work continues: to explore the potential "future (s)" of our denomination. Embedded in the MVS language was the potential for plural futures, and since that document was drafted in the weeks following the 2016 General Conference, the possibility that we could not walk together, or that we needed more space, existed even then.

The recurring use of the words "as possible" - the call to maximize the witness in as many places in the world as possible and to seek as much contextual differentiation as possible and as much unity as possible - was understood as acknowledging this to be an open question.

There was also in the MVS document a dissatisfaction with the status quo and a desire for newness: new ways of embodying unity, new ways of being in relationship, and new forms and structures of relationship.

It is important *that* we use the language of "new" and *how* we use the language of "new."

There needs to be sufficient newness to create space for inclusion, freedom, and conscience. This was the spirit of the One Church Plan, which had the majority of support of the Council of Bishops, the U. S. members of the Commission on a Way Forward, and the U.S. delegates to the Special Session.

The conversations happening across the church are in search of this newness. Again, conversation is the currency of change, and more conversation is better than less. Conversations are happening in each central conference and jurisdiction and within and across progressive, centrist, and traditional mindsets.

The conversations will necessarily flow into public spaces,

including the 2020 General Conference. The wider the participation in these conversations, the better. And yet alongside conversation, the real life of the church continues. Several behaviors are possible, and they are not mutually exclusive:

- **To live** as if we are a church of the One Church Plan.

- **To recognize** less unity is possible and more space is needed.

- **To design a way of being the church** that redefines connectionality through greater local freedom and autonomy (*Book of Discipline*, p.125).

This is our urgent task: to redefine our present connectionality. We have the harm that the *BOD* does to the LGBTQIA+ community. This was named earlier in the COB pastoral letter (December, 2018) prior to the Special Session, by speakers and observers at the Special Session, and afterward in full page advertisements, statements by clergy and laity in annual conferences, and in testimonies that have expressed conscience, differentiation, and resistance.

There is a need for conversation that leads to the redefinition of structure. The work on a General Book of Discipline holds promise, as does the possibility of a more uniform capacity to adapt the *Book of Discipline* across our regions and continents, and the need for the U.S. to become a central conference, for the sake of contextualization. There is renewed attention to the Connectional Conference Plan. Structure is important, for it enables the provisions and protections that are essential for the flourishing of individuals and communities.

## Epilogue: Faithfulness, Unity, and Fruitfulness

As an elder and bishop, I have stood many times at an altar and raised my hands to God and said the words of the epiclesis, the invocation of the Holy Spirit present in the bread and cup that we receive, and then repeated the aspiration that we will actually be the body of Christ for the world. And then the powerful appeal to God:

*Make us one with Christ—this is faithfulness,*
*make us one with each other—this is unity,*
*and make us one in ministry to all the world—this is fruitfulness.*

The Holy Spirit does sustain leaders through a complex season. There remains for all of us a charge to keep, a God to glorify. I pray that we remain in communion with each other. Since my installation as president of the Council of Bishops, I have often found myself in churches, kneeling at altars, praying for the faithfulness, unity, and fruitfulness of the church. These are linked together and form a whole. We cannot be one without abiding in Jesus. We cannot be spirit-filled without loving our neighbor. We cannot experience revival as we sow divisions in the body.

And so, we continue to pray: May God give us the will and the discernment for a way beyond the Way Forward.

**Ken Carter** is president of the Council of Bishops and resident bishop of the Florida Area. He was a moderator of the Commission on a Way Forward and is author of Embracing the Wideness of God's Mercy (Abingdon).

# CHAPTER SEVEN

# Alex da Silva Souto
## Our Movement Forward

Yesterday, I witnessed a holy coming out. Just beyond the front doors of the parsonage, I spotted the first crocus of the season. There it was: tiny and simple in form but flaunting its majestic purple. This morning, my ears were treated to the song of an enthusiastic little bird, prophesying that spring is on the way. As I reflect on the current realities and the future of our denomination, as well as my own place in the order of things, these are the signs and wonders I have been trying to hold on to: the boldness of the flower and promise of the song.

Recent fall and winter seasons have been brutal. I have not experienced relentlessly cold temperatures like these since I moved out of a San Francisco apartment with the flimsiest windows, and no heating system. I wish this last year was only painful due to harsh weather. Unfortunately, it has been additionally agonizing because it has also marked the ending of the United Methodist denomination as we know it. On a personal level, this experience has been something akin to watching my father's body fall apart before my eyes. The doctors tried to do what they could. Perhaps more could have been done, but the combination of diseases afflicting his body were ultimately ruthless and fatal. Sadly, the same seems to be true for our denomination. A lethal combination of long-term systemic diseases have taken their toll on the body known as The United Methodist Church (UMC).

Plenty of people still claim that our denomination is not yet dead, and that another round of chemotherapy (i.e. General Conferences 2020, 2024, 2028) might do the trick of healing this broken body. Others are in even deeper denial. They argue for lesser remedies in hopes that all "our troubles" will eventually fade away if we just practice patience with "hearts at peace." To all who are working to keep the church alive, I am with you. To all who are fighting to keep the institution alive as it is, I ask: How much more abuse (legislative, physical, and spiritual) can this denominational body take? How many more decades of institutionalism, politicking, and branding strategies are we willing to endure while discriminated, marginalized, and criminalized lives are unremittingly to be thrown under the bus? For many of us, it is beyond time to go back to being the transformative movement we once were. Our reality is perfectly described by prophet Jeremiah:

> **"They have treated the wound of my people carelessly, saying, 'Peace, peace,' when there is no peace."**
>
> **~Jeremiah 6:14 (NRSV)**

It feels like a hopeless flashback, or a purgatory version of *Groundhog Day*.[1] This last year has been equivalent to some of my CPE[2] days... There I am, standing in the corner of the emergency room, watching doctors pounding on the chest of a lifeless body, or next to a hospital bed as a family is informed of the impending demise of a loved one. Yes, it is indeed a grim scenario, beloved siblings in Christ! Sadly, more "chemotherapy" (General Conferences) or newly proposed "amputation surgeries" (pushing out or buying out one group or another) will not save this denominational body. Whichever treatment plan is followed, any measure based on wishful thinking certainly would not be the best or most faithful response.

Conversely, the truth of a "correct diagnosis" can set us free. The cruel reality is that our denomination – this human institution – is as perishable as any living thing, and it is not long for this world. However, it is also true that the church is as eternal as the Spirit is eternal. A queer clergy colleague of mine, who is currently under charges (i.e. ecclesial terror) has taught me that there is a fundamental difference between the UMC as "a denomination" or institution, and the UMC as "a church."

This distinction has helped me better cope with the death of our denomination as we know it. Similar to the prophetic song of this morning's little bird, the 1972 hymn, "We Are the Church" by Donald Marsh becomes tune when sorrow overcomes me, and it has been keeping my faith alive:

---

[1] The character played by Bill Murray keeps living the same day over and over again. Clip: "Groundhog Day (1993)," IMDB.com, accessed April 12, 2019, https://www.imdb.com/title/tt0107048/. Murray, Bill. *Groundhog Day*. Directed by Harold Ramis. Los Angeles: Columbia, 1993.

[2] Clinical Pastoral Education.

*The church is not a building,*
*the church is not a steeple,*
*the church is not a resting place,*
*the church is a people.* [3]

The UMC as a denomination may have collapsed under the weight of its own (neo)colonialist history, institutional priorities, patriarchal dispositions, and white-privileged tendencies, but the church– The Methodist Movement – is still alive. Perhaps hindered and harmed by decades of systemic afflictions, yet it is still alive because the Church is eternal, just as the Holy Spirit is eternal.

As far as I can tell, John Wesley never wanted to start a new denomination, and neither did Martin Luther, nor Jesus Christ for that matter. Was it not, and is it not, all about the Church being a collective of people simply and faithfully practicing unconditional love, justice, collective liberation, and grace? The Christian Spirit – the Church – has survived waves of institutional deaths, revisions, and reformations. It is beyond time we acknowledge the gravity of where we are as a denomination, otherwise we cannot move forward.

There will be no revival, resurrection, or a future without first admitting and experiencing the realities of this day and the death of our deeply broken system. There is life to be had on the other side of death, for life is not its opposite, but the thread that runs from before birth, all the way through death.

> **"Very truly, I tell you, unless a grain of wheat falls into the earth and dies, it remains just a single grain; but if it dies, it bears much fruit."**
>
> **John 12:24 (NRSV)**

The spirit of the Church is deeply wounded as the Body of Christ is deeply wounded; but it is eternal and, therefore, shall prevail. Why aren't more of us focusing on the potentiality of this moment and the reality of eternal life, instead of trying to revive a defunct and clearly overburdened structure? Is the delusion of "institutional unity" above all else worth the cost? Our denominational body may have succumbed to the systemic evils of institutionalism,

---

[3] Marsh, Donald and Richard Avery. *We Are the Church. The United Methodist Hymnal* #558: 1989. https://www.hopepublishing.com/find-hymns-hw/hw4145.aspx.

47

(neo)colonialism, white supremacy, racism, sexism, homophobia, transphobia, and heterosexism, amongst other evils, but the Spirit of the Church is yet alive.

I beg your mindful reading, and share the real concerns regarding the survival of our global agencies, commissions, and boards. With that said, no way forward exists to preserve the global structure as it is and, at the same time, address the harsh and unsustainable realities of our denominational fractures. How can we move conscientiously forward with a body that is so abused, shattered, or even dead, as some would attest?

For the last seven years I have been involved with a connectional partnership between faithful siblings from the Mozambique and New York Annual Conferences (NYAC). This fruitful relationship was started twenty years ago by a couple who are members of my local church. What started as an academically funded trip two decades ago has become a long-standing ministerial partnership. It grew from being a local church effort to becoming a ministry sustained through various annual conference(s) efforts and GBGM (General Board of Global Ministries) investments.

As I write this paragraph, UMCOR (United Methodist Committee on Relief) is working diligently on recovery efforts after cyclone Idai devastated large parts of Mozambique, Malawi, and parts of Zimbabwe. This tragic event raises questions about the demand for, and feasibility of, global ministries if the denomination ceases to exist as we know it. Could we not find ways to sustain UMCOR without the current UMC structure?

The Acción Médica Cristiana in Nicaragua is another fruitful international partnership deeply close to my heart. This is not a UMC organization, but it is an entity vetted by the Advance program of GBGM that employs a North American GBGM missionary. This ministerial partnership transcends UMC denominational structures and ties, and it may serve as a wonderful model for future global partnerships independent from the UMC superstructure. Along the same line, my local church has sent members to work in Puerto Rico as part of Disaster Response teams. Puerto Rico has a concordat relationship with The United Methodist Church, yet we have been able to work collaboratively. UMCOR plays a role, but the work transcends UMC bonds. This partnership is a fruit of our annual conference signing a Memorandum of Understanding with the Methodist Church in Puerto Rico in 2018.

Additionally, there are prolific, long-standing mission partnerships between NYAC churches and other Caribbean countries independent of UMC affiliation. Why can we not continue our work of mutual support and global solidarity for the "transformation of the world" through a thoughtfully considered reconfiguration or a new expression of Methodism (if resurrection demands it)? Humanitarian and capacity-building efforts should never be predicated on denominational affiliation. We serve and partner beyond denominational boundaries because the Church transcends the logo on the front of the buildings and the cover of our hymnals.

GBCS (General Board of Church and Society), GBHEM (General Board of Higher Education and Ministry), GCORR (General Commission on Religion and Race), and UMW (United Methodist Women) are more complex questions, and I might need an additional chapter or an entire new book to address them. For now, I contend that our connectional work requires re-envisioning if we are to move forward. It needs to be a grassroots movement as opposed to a task force for the preservation of the status-quo, or re-organizing without systemic change. Keep the good DNA, but a new body is in order.

Prior to General Conference 2019, the only way forward for me was the Simple Plan. I believed then, and still believe now, that it was the only compromise that could have preserved a degree of theological integrity and rescued the moral grounding of our denomination. Eliminating all discriminatory and punitive language against the LGBTQIA+ community[4] from the *BoD* (*Book of Discipline*) would have allowed us to preserve our connectionalism and move into institutional revision, while giving ourselves another chance to sort out fundamental discrepancies.

In contrast, I believed that the other plans before General Conference would inevitably cause the collapse of our connectional system – whether through the increased discrimination and punishment, as proposed by the Traditionalist Plan, or the overly complex re-structuring of the Connectional Conference Plan without addressing the root causes of the harms perpetrated by our denomination, or the theological and moral compromise of the One Church Plan. Collapse and the urgency of now is what many of us are experiencing! Are we going down the Niagara River while pretending we are on solid ground?

---

[4] Lesbian, Gay, Bisexual Transgender, Queer, Intersex, Asexual, the "+" symbol stands for sexual orientations and gender identities beyond this acronym.

## The Niagara River

Kay Ryan, 1945[5]

As though
the river were
a floor, we position
our table and chairs
upon it,
eat,
and have conversation.
As it moves along,
we notice—
as calmly as though
dining room paintings
were being replaced—
the changing scenes
along the shore.
We do know,
we do know
this is the Niagara River,
but
it is hard to remember
what that means.

The Traditionalist Plan is a disorder. Its destructive cells were implanted within the Body of Christ known as the UMC when the Institute on Religion and Democracy (IRD) focused their hate-filled strategies on us, as one of the major denominations practicing the social gospel. The morally ambiguous and theologically compromised One Church Plan, would have locked us on the path of regionalization of identity-based discrimination and, therefore, denominational fragmentation. I hear the good intentions and believe in the kindness of heart of its proponents and the ones who still believe in this privileged compromise, but it was far from being the solution

[5] From *The Niagara River* by Kay Ryan, published by Grove Press. Copyright © 2005 by Kay Ryan.

that could have saved us or our denomination. The multifarious re-structuring proposed by the Connectional Conference Plan was a convoluted "plan of treatment" that would have inevitably led to dismembering connectional parts without addressing the actual systemic evils plaguing the UMC. However, some influential UMC leaders are taking a second look at it, trying to find lessons on schism as either the inevitable consequence of decades of the meta-phorical chemotherapy, or the cause of the death of our denomination as we know it.

Rev. Dr. Ted. A. Campbell, from Perkins School of Theology has argued that "we are divided" and that "we need a degree of sepa-ration."[6] Even though he does not argue for the creation of a new structure called 'connectional conference,' he seems to be interested in "[remaining connected]" as a concept found in the Connectional Conference Plan. Generally speaking, I appreciate Rev. Campbell's line of thinking and practical suggestions, but the most valuable aspect of his argument is the list of Methodist essentials that could help preserve, or restore, our connectionalism across the globe: the Articles of Religion and the Confession of Faith, the General Rules, and Wesley's *Standard Sermons*. Rev. Campbell also suggests the preservation of "specific social teachings (like opposition to slavery and other forms of human trafficking) that should be specified at a global level."

I concur wholeheartedly with the preservation of those Wesleyan foundations, but I would add that universal human dignity and the sacred worth of all beings are also essential social teachings neces-sary to maintain the theological and moral fabric of our connec-tionalism. The concept of sacred worth is found in the *BoD*, but it remains a mere concept when identity-based discrimination is a tangible component of our denominational teachings and practices. Is Campbell suggesting that the full inclusion and affirmation of LGBTQIA+ people are part of the "non-essentials" in the re-envision-ing of our denomination?

If that is the case, Campbell's statements are consistent with the compromises of the One Church and Connectional Conference Plans. The maxim: "In essentials, unity; in non-essentials, liberty; in all things, charity" was so often thrown around that one would have thought that it was said by Jesus Christ himself. This dictum is erroneously attributed to St. Augustine, but it is of much later origin. It is traced to Rupertus Meldenius appearing for the first

---

[6] "An Ash Wednesday Mediation," Heartcore Methodist, March 6, 2019, https://www. facebook.com/notes/heartcore-methodist/an-ash-wednesday-meditation-envision-ing-a-central-conference-plan-for-united-met/817019445322856/.

time in Germany, A.D. 1627 and 1628, among Lutheran and German Reformed churches, and then popularized by moderates in England during that same century.[7] Granted, the principle of unity in essentials and tolerance in non-essentials exerted a significant influence on John Wesley's writing. However, one could argue that when it came to social justice matters, Wesley and early Methodists up to the twentieth century were not exactly known as centrists, moderates, or complacent in any way, shape, or form. Is there really a "centrist" or "moderate" position in matters of justice? I can see being a centrist in partisanship battles, but the current UMC struggle is between a dominant group and a group simply seeking to exist within the full life of the church. There is no neutral zone for anybody to occupy. One is either in solidarity with the marginalized, or one is in collaboration with the party doing the marginalizing. The claim that there is a "broad center" ambivalent to the questions of injustice in our denomination furthers a false equivalency between those on either side of this fictive "middle ground." To make matters worse, the ones who are members of the LGBTQIA+ community and our allies continue to be labeled "incompatibilists" if we are not willing to acquiesce to the continuation of identity-based discrimination.

This reinforces the marginalization of progressives on the left, insinuating that our aim is to control what others think and do, rather than simply being allowed to exist and fully participate in the life of the church. It might be more accurate to say that, in the UMC, marginalized groups are the ones stuck in the middle, between white supremacists on one side and white saviors on the other. Ultimately, human dignity, sacred worth, and justice are indisputable essentials. Liberty in non-essentials is an effective principle for de-escalation of conflict, but when it is mindlessly applied or misappropriated to justify identity-based discrimination, it has the side effect of creating an environment of domination at best, and a tyranny of the majority at worst.

More often than not, the dominating party "gaslights" the minority group, asserting that what is essential to them is non-essential to the common good. Currently, fundamentalists on the right, centrists, and even some privileged progressives gaslight the LGBTQIA+ community asserting our discrimination, criminalization, and punishment is not that bad, and that our advocacy for affirmation in the full life of the church is a non-essential. "Why can't we just 'agree to disagree' and move on to more important ecclesial and theological matters," they

---

[7] "A common quotation from 'Augustine?,'" Georgetown Faculty, accessed April 12, 2019, http://faculty.georgetown.edu/jod/augustine/quote.html.

ask. However, by refuting the essential rights of LGBTQIA+ people in the UMC, misrepresenting our legitimate claims, denying that acts of injustice are actually occurring, and further marginalizing us, the majority group is reasserting its privilege and dominance.

Unfortunately, the concept of "maximization of contextualization" has also been misappropriated to justify injustices and majority biases. Both the One Church Plan and the Connectional Conference Plan drew heavily on arguments for "maximization of contextualization." When applied to matters of social justice, what is meant to be a tool for the advancement of liberty and de-colonization becomes a machination for situational ethics and moral relativism.[8]

When what is deemed the prevalent "context" is determined by the majority without regards for the well-being of a minority, "contextualization" is no longer a force for good but a tool for practices of suppression, oppression, erasure, and domination. Human dignity and sacred worth should be viewed as universal values independent of what may be deemed as the prevalent "cultural context." No human being or group of people should be prevented from entering into the full life of the Church simply because of their identity.

Being a member of the LGBTQIA+ community is still taboo in many cultures and a crime in a significant number of countries throughout our connection. In some, it is even punishable by death. Albeit a changing reality, it is still a challenging reality. While I don't expect United Methodists to start civil wars in those countries to change those inhumane laws, don't our baptismal vows demand that we resist evil in all its forms? It is precisely because of the criminalization and punishment of members of the LGBTQIA+ community in countries where the UMC is highly influential that we have to decide once and for all whether it is homosexuality or homophobia/heterosexism that is an evil.

We cannot have it both ways. We cannot continue to make allowances (and excuses) for the condemnation of LGBTQIA+ people, and at the same time claim that we uphold the human dignity and sacred worth of all persons. The continued criminalization and punishment of the LGBTQIA+ community, or ambiguity about our sacred worth and human dignity, only favors the systemic harm done unto us, our families, and our allies. If we know that a minority is harmed solely due to their identity, we have a Christian mandate to speak up against it and remain in solidarity with the marginalized, especially

---

[8] For more in point, refer to: "Ain't I a Christian?," UM-forward.org, accessed April 12, 2019, https://um-forward.org/our-stories/2018/8/24/aint-i-a-christian-theological-moral-and-ecclesiological-ground-of-the-simple-plan.

if the origin of such discrimination, criminalization, and punishment is directly traced to our doctrinal prejudices.

The violence against LGBTQIA+ people around the world is a product of misguided beliefs and theological corruption propagated by fundamentalists. We have to denounce those corrupt doctrines if we are to see a reduction in crimes against our LGBTQIA+ community. Civil laws on their own cannot protect the lives of queer people anywhere if religious institutions continue to proclaim that we are incompatible, sinners, or abominations, simply because we are honest about our God-given identities.

Brazil, my own country of birth, has one of the best systems of legal protections for the LGBQTIA+ community. Yet, reports show that on average one trans person is killed a day, and violence against the community still runs rampant. Even worse, the swelling fundamentalist movement in Brazil is now seeking to reverse federal civil rights protections for the LGBQTIA+ community. Sadly, the threat to civil rights in Brazil seems to follow the trend of the far-right movement in the U.S., seeking to undermine and/or reverse civil rights protections for LGBTQIA+ people, women, racial/ethnic minorities, and economically oppressed persons.

If homophobia and heterosexism is an invention of biased religious authorities, it is reasonable to expect that religious communities are ultimately charged with dismantling these death-dealing biases. Even centrists and right-of-center people who may dwell in theological conundrums regarding the affirmation and protection of LGBTQIA+ individuals, have the moral mandate to speak against discrimination, criminalization, and punishment of our community from at least a humanitarian and ethical perspective. And that cannot be done through convenient, yet irresponsible ambiguities, false equivalences, and expectations that civil laws will do the work of changing hearts and minds if our doctrines work to inspire and incite the dehumanization of under-represented groups.

There is a direct correlation between what our denomination teaches about a particular group and the violence against such group, despite the intended protections of civil laws. Therefore, it is beyond time we correct our teachings to align with what brings life, instead of what instigates and causes harm, too often to the point of death. Can this change be accomplished through our denomination's legislative process? I have lost hope of that. The General Conference system has been deeply corrupted and dominated by the fundamentalist far-right, and for too long, undermined by the complacency of the privileged ones. We need a bold and unequivocal proclamation that all identity-based discrimination, criminalization, and punishment is contrary to Christian teaching and that we will no longer be content with and/or accommodating of such practices.

Unfortunately, many denominational leaders are primarily concerned with the management of a public relations crisis, not the fundamental questions of systemic evils and covert/overt prejudices inherent in our denominational structure and practices. It pains me to witness the continual use of God's resources (financial and human) for the preservation of institutional games and power trips, instead of investing in dismantling systems of oppression.

As the Holy Scriptures say, if we are to have new wine, we better get some new wineskins. What does this new wineskin look like? In my mind, this new wineskin is of a "highly melanined" shade because the "master's tools will never dismantle the master's house," as Audre Lorde prophetically stated.[9] We need a new expression of Methodism to come from the ones on the margins, not from those at the center of institutional power. Anything less than that runs the risk of replicating the very system that favors the already privileged ones. If PoC+Q+T (People of Color+Queer+Trans)[10] communities lead the way, we are more likely to avoid the root causes that led these identities to be discriminated against, criminalized, and punished in the first place.

If the collapse of our denominational body was due to the systemic evils of institutionalism, (neo)colonialism, white supremacy, racism, sexism, homophobia, transphobia, and heterosexism, the very individuals targeted by these evils might have a thing or two to say about a new wineskin, a new vision, and recovery of the principles of our original movement. One thing is absolutely certain: there is an eminent desire for a new wine that will lead to the restoration of our movement. However, in order for this restoration, revival, or full on re-birth to happen, we must first come to grips with our grim realities and our historical failings. There can be no reconciliation without first repentance and sharing of the truth.

Therefore, the future must come from the margins, for the margin is where the movement began. History teaches us that the religious powers that be had never grasped the revolutionary nature of the Christ movement, nor the Methodist movement, but the ordinary people and most certainly the marginalized people did. Within the UMC, the powers that be have known of the systemic evils and injustices of our denomination for decades but still continuously

---

[9] From the essay of the same name, included in Sister Outsider. "Audre Lorde Biography," Biography.com, April 1, 2013, https://www.biography.com/people/audre-lorde-214108.

[10] The "+" symbol connotes the variations of these underrepresented identities.

choose institutional and self-preservation over stopping the harm and living out the social gospel.

Weren't the Simple Rules, the Social Gospel, and the Quadrilateral the bone marrow of the Methodist movement before we became so consumed with building and maintaining an institution? It is time to go back to the basics, to the simple acts of "loving God above all things and our neighbors as ourselves." A courageous queer clergy sibling of mine signs her emails with a quotation by Kate Marvel that reads:

> *"We don't need hope... we only need*
> *courage to do what needs doing."*

The prophet Micah has taught us what we need to be doing:

**Do justice, and to love kindness, and**
**to walk humbly with your God.**

**Micah 6:8 (NRSV)**

Thanks be to God for the ones keeping the Christ Movement alive, even if that means acknowledging our denominational deaths so that the Church can live as the Christ Movement springs up again. For love is the fruit and the labor of impossibilities.

**Rev. Alex da Silva Souto** has been a person of the "in between space" since his birth and childhood in Brazil. After living in Japan for nearly two years, he moved to San Francisco, California where he served as a lay leader in the California/Nevada Annual Conference. He transferred his membership to NYAC during his studies at Yale Divinity School. He is currently the Senior Pastor of the New Milford United Methodist Church in Connecticut and a devoted social justice advocate through the collective efforts of UM*Forward*.

# CHAPTER EIGHT
## Talbot Davis

To Redefine our Present Connectionality:
Thoughts on a Way Beyond the Way Forward

I write these words as a United Methodist elder serving in a modern church holding what has come to be called the traditional sexual ethic. I support the traditional teaching of celibacy in single-ness and faithfulness in heterosexual marriage for three reasons:

1. Conversation within Scripture allows for conversation beyond it. Such is the case with slavery and women's ordination. Consensus within Scripture implies obedience beyond it. Such is the case with homosexual intercourse. I find it especially interesting that, when Jesus could have redefined marriage in Matthew 19, he reinforced it instead.

2. In addition to the unanimity of the biblical witness, the church for all time and all around the globe has affirmed the definition of marriage and the standards for both human sexuality and ordina-tion as described in #1 above.

3. These matters ARE in fact <u>essentials</u> of the faith for three reasons: a) Paul connects his theology of resurrection in I Corin-thians 15 with his theology of the body in the rest of the book; b) Marriage is the first institution God creates and is the final meta-phor he brings for the world to come. Surely those biblical book-ends imply something about how we understand all that comes in between; c) Unlike all the areas on which there is an "agree to disagree" mindset in the church, this is the only one in which that disagreement would be "liturgicalized" into the life of the church: weddings of homosexual couples and ordination of partnered homosexual persons.

A generation ago, Alanis Morissette asked all of us to consider the question, "Isn't it ironic?" The song had a great hook, a memo-rable video, and a penetrating lyric in which the singer answers her own question, "And isn't it ironic, don't you think; A little too ironic, and yeah I really do think." [1]

And as we United Methodists consider "Where Are We Now?" on the way to establishing "Where Do We Go From Here?" Morissette's words ring as true today as they did in the 90s, for we find ourselves in a place of rich irony. I believe that understanding the irony of our present state is a necessary and painful prelude to diagnosing a possible move from irony to clarity.

## WHERE ARE WE NOW?

The irony we live in manifests itself in at least the four following ways.

### 1.It Is A Self-Made Crisis.

Writing in late 2016, Rev. James Howell, the pastor of Myers Park UMC in my hometown of Charlotte and a vocal supporter of both the Uniting Methodists and the One Church Plan, painted this dystopian picture of the future of the congregation he serves if it ever had to make a choice between a "Conservative" United Methodist denomination and a "Progressive" one:

> Of the 3,600 [active members], I'd imagine 1,400 would rally to the progressive side, and about 1,000 would go conservative. Or maybe it would be roughly a tie. Or maybe 1,400 to 1,000 the other way. What would happen to the "losers"? Of course, the remaining 1,200 would be too disgusted to vote at all. Our young adults would, quite simply, be done with us.

> Many — several dozen, I'd estimate — would exit and become Southern Baptist, or Episcopalians. I'd suspect that many more, though, in the hundreds, would just give up on church altogether if the one they loved and trusted couldn't do any better than this sorry state of affairs. And I would not blame one of them. Families would be divided over which way to go. A 5,200-member church gutted, with maybe 1,500 left.

> We would quickly have to lay off two-thirds of our staff and hack our mission spending down to a small fraction of what it's been. Within months, a clinic in Haiti would

---

[1] Morissette, Alanis and Glen Ballard. Ironic. Reprise Records, 1995.

shut down; families moving out of homelessness would head back to the streets. We'd be the laughingstock of Charlotte. The new conference of the new denomination wouldn't even be all that glad to have us, as we'd have so little money left to send in.

### Dogs and cats living together!

Still, as I read those words in 2016 and re-read them now, my reaction is the same: "James, this is a cause you have chosen, a crisis you have created, an ancient, global, consensual teaching of the church that you have sought to overhaul. Why the lament for the dilemma you have caused?"

Now: Dr. Howell's situation is not unique among the UMC's more progressive wing and its highest profile proponents of the One Church Plan. Yet, he is the only one to go so public with such a Metho-Dystopian view *well ahead of our current apocalypse.* There would be no Showdown At Myers Park, there would be no denominational impasse, there would be no current volume for which I am contributing this chapter if a large swath of the denomination had decided long ago: *We are not smarter than Paul. We're not more enlightened than Augustine. Newer isn't better, younger isn't smarter, and this Gospel we have received has consistently maintained that marriage is for one man and one woman and in the sacredness of that context alone is where God blesses sexual intimacy.*

But such has not been the case. Instead, we are faced with a situation in which the sexual revisionists among us declare, "I have a problem! What are YOU going to do about it?" That intersection of irony and codependency is one I am loathed to enter.

### 2. MMAA.

We find a second layer of post General Conference irony in the unsubtle attempts by those who lost the vote regarding the One Church and Traditional Plans to *Make Methodism American Again.* In the words of Mark Holland of *Mainstream UMC*[2]: "It is becoming increasingly clear that the U.S. church is ready for new life."

The cat has officially left the bag. I find it … *a little too ironic …* that the same colleagues who have long listed diversity among the church's most urgent goals now discover their goal has

---

[2] Holland, Mark, "Key African Leader Calls for Split in UMC," MainstreamUMC.com, accessed April 15, 2019, https://mainstreamumc.com/blog/key-african-leader-calls-for-split-in-umc/

become their obstacle. If people *look* different from us but *think* like us, that's diversity. If they *look* different <u>and</u> *think* differently, that's oppression.

In the richest of all the MMAA ironies, the Reconciling Ministries Network attributed the success of the Traditional Plan at General Conference '19 to a *"white nationalist strain of Christianity."* Such an assessment would no doubt be news to the continental Africans making up much of the coalition that supported the Traditional Plan, as well as the members of more than 40 nations who worship at Good Shepherd on a typical Sunday. Well, it's like Jesus always said, *"Then you shall know the truth and define it geographically."*

### 3. We Have The Toys, But No Batteries.

The final irony in our current situation falls back on me and my like-minded, globally conservative friends. We "own" the apparatus of the denomination but have no ability to operate it. By that I mean we have the official endorsement of our foundational teaching documents, we have the voting coalition to ensure that it prevails long into the future, but we have very few annual conferences, bishops, or even district superintendents who will implement what we say we are. I therefore find myself in the position of remaining in a church body that believes as I do in the matter of human sexuality, the definition of marriage, and standards for ordination ... yet is incapable of behaving in accord with its stated beliefs.

Even though the conservative globalists "won" a battle of General Conference 2019, in most cases, we lack the local administrative clout to enforce the peace. We have prevented what I would call "codified heresy" – a redefinition of marriage in some places that would, by definition, redefine it in all places – yet remain powerless to stop our superiors and colleagues from proceeding unimpeded with their ministry of redefinition. Ironic, indeed – and in this case, depressingly so.

### 4. Whither E Pluribus Unum?

In the lead up to General Conference, the rallying cry of those in support of the One Church Plan was, *"Unity!"* As soon as the plan failed, many of the same voices are now declaring, *"Separation!"* What happened?

It's simple: *the definition of "unity" changed the minute the teaching of the church didn't.*

Isn't it ironic?

So that's where we are: a place rich with irony and thick with ambiguity. Yet, I very much prefer this state to the alternative. I believe that General Conference 2019 protected Methodism from itself. We protected the faith handed down, once and for all, to the saints. We maintained a tight connection between our Christology and our Sexology.

> **"Because the stakes are high. The slippery
> slope does exist. Not among our laity."**

Shockingly, among our clergy. If you doubt me, see these words in a March, 2016 publication from the Methodist Federation For Social Action, an anonymous post that made even the most jaded among us blush. Titled "#HandsOffMyBC" and authored by a United Methodist clergyperson, the blog made an emphatic case for universal access to birth control while also including these stunning admissions:

> "I chose to go on birth control because I didn't want to get pregnant and I wanted to have sex. Because I am a clergy woman in The United Methodist Church, and I'm single, that information could get me brought up on charges, and I could lose my ordination.

> Luckily, I can access birth control through the health insurance plan that my church pays for. However, because I value my job, I have to remain anonymous in writing this. It strikes me as ridiculous in 2016 that this is necessary, but being a person who is sexually active while single is against the rules."

Not drop the mic. Drop the jaw. Yet tame when compared to that which appeared in the Comments section, most notably from an aspiring ordinand in Oklahoma:

> "Hi there. Future UMC Rev. here (starting seminary this fall.) Thank you so much for this brave post. Your body, your sexuality, and your safety are your decisions and I applaud you for your willingness to share, even anonymously. My fiancé and I (he's going to be a Rev. too) started having sex a couple of years ago and were thrilled with our decision, and it wasn't one we made lightly, as I'm sure you don't take sexual activity lightly. As for the promises of ordination...perhaps it's time to

take a second look at those."

So, this is what it has come to: a pair of would-be UMC ordinands inviting us to celebrate their premarital sexual intercourse. Just when I thought I'd seen it all, I realize I hadn't.

Note the perspective in both Anonymous' post and the referenced comment. It's the church of "me" and of "now." It's an ecclesiology wrapped up in personal autonomy. It's a faith in which the highest allegiance is to the self. It's a hermeneutic which confuses "rules" with "commandments" and mistakes "historic" for "obsolete."

It's a future for The United Methodist Church in which sacrifice-making, cross-taking, self-denying holiness has gone the way of garters and petticoats. And that is the future, ironic or not, from which the General Conference 2019 protected The United Methodist Church.

## Where Do We Go From Here?

To put it another way: *What does the journey from irony to clarity look like?* I have three suggestions (don't worry, no poem at the end).

### 1. Don't Confuse Doctrine with Strategy.

As a denomination, we officially believe and teach celibacy in singleness and faithfulness in heterosexual marriage. For that, I give praises to God because at the intersection of his wisdom and his beauty, God invented sex AND gave us its boundaries. As Matt O'Reilly says, *"the vulnerability of sex requires the safety of marriage."* So, that's what we have inherited, what we treasure, and what we teach.

Yet, we should never suggest that such a doctrine then demands a strategy of rejection towards those who identify as LGBTQIA+. All I can do is say what happens at the church I serve, Good Shepherd UMC in Charlotte, North Carolina. A number of years ago, I received an email from a same-gendered female couple asking if they'd be welcomed at Good Shepherd. I decided to reply via a phone call instead of by email, and in that conversation assured the questioners they'd be warmly welcomed, while also letting them know what we teach. I told them that I wanted them to come, but wasn't going to give them a *bait and switch*. They appreciated the honesty, came the next day, and thoroughly enjoyed the experience. After several Sundays, one of the couple said to me, "We really like the way you all teach the Bible. All we were getting at our (MCC-type church) was Bible-lite." Ironic, don't ya think?

We have some people at Good Shepherd who surrender their

same-sex impulses to God for the sake of the kingdom and live celibate lives. We have others who don't make that choice. (Of course,
as any pastor will tell you, we have more than enough trauma from
straight sex issues in the church to keep all pastoral staff busy until
we hear the voice of the archangel and the trumpet call of God.) We
do our best to communicate in a loving way that God's design for us
is to surrender our impulses so we don't surrender to them.

## 2. Exchange Holy Conversations for Honest Declarations.

Can we use General Conference 2019 as the occasion where we
officially declare an end to the era of "Holy Conversations?" Those
talks seldom proved holy and generally took the form of a lecture
rather than dialog. Most of us who lean right theologically long
assumed that "Holy Conversation" was really code for "you stay
here long enough and I will eventually talk you into changing your
mind." On some occasions, that's exactly what happened. On many
more occasions, mutual frustration was the end result, never with
more clarity than in St. Louis.

Instead, I recommend moving to a season of *Honest Declarations*.
Our situation at Good Shepherd – a congregation in the same city
with similar attendance numbers as Dr. Howell's Myers Park UMC
I referenced earlier in the chapter – might be a case in point. In the
run-up to General Conference 2019, we had NO church-wide conversations on either the impending vote or the matter of homosexuality
and the church. We had two reasons for such a strategy:

1. We assumed that the Traditional Plan would pass, leaving us
in precisely the same kind of denomination post-GC as we were
pre-GC, so why heighten anxiety over something that might not
even happen (and, as it turned out, didn't)?

2. We have long had clarity in our printed materials, our spoken
sermons, and our church workshops regarding what we believe
and teach to be God's design for human sexuality: celibacy in
singleness and faithfulness in heterosexual marriage. As a
result, we had none of the recommended church-wide listening
sessions asking, "Well, what's YOUR opinion?" We decided not to
spend one moment discerning what we believe God has long ago
decided.

That combination of low anxiety and high clarity has led to zero
fallout from General Conference 2019. The decision reinforcing
what the UMC has always believed about marriage, sexuality,

and ordination was greeted with sighs of relief by the few who
were paying attention and blissful ignorance by the majority
who weren't. Like any congregation, we do many things poorly at
Good Shepherd, but this was one decision that worked well. Here
is a portion of what our Board sent to Western North Carolina's
voting delegation as the GC approached:

> We love being a United Methodist Church. We are grate-
> ful for the support in our early years as a congregation,
> we value relationships across our connection, and in
> this season of our church's life, we are honored to be a
> resource to other churches and other leaders.

> We also align ourselves with the doctrinal heritage of
> United Methodism and its strong embrace of salvation by
> grace, free will, assurance of salvation, and holiness that
> is both personal and social.

> Among the doctrines we appreciate about United Method-
> ism has been its unwavering affirmation that marriage
> is designed by God to consist of one man and one woman.
> Further, sexual intimacy is blessed by God only within the
> confines of heterosexual marriage. We find it particularly
> compelling that in Matthew 19, when Jesus could have
> redefined marriage, he reinforced it instead.

> We further support the long-standing Methodist doctrine
> and language regarding homosexual individuals and
> homosexual practice: that while all are people of sacred
> worth, the practice of homosexuality is incompatible
> with Christian teaching.

> As a congregation, we stand with Christians for all time
> and in all parts of the globe in declaring that God has
> a beautiful design for sexuality, introduced in Genesis
> 2 and woven through the rest of the biblical library:
> one man and one woman in relational love that reflects
> Christ's love for the church. Because of that global,
> historic, and biblical affirmation, we believe that homo-
> sexual romance and intercourse is not God's design for
> his people.

> For these reasons we cannot support the One Church
> Plan. While we laud its calls for unity and its respect
> for pastoral conscience, we believe it makes The United

Methodist Church abandon historic, global orthodoxy as it re-defines marriage and re-imagines qualifications for ordained ministry. It asks us to believe that there are two competing and contradictory orthodoxies for marriage, sex, and ordination. This we cannot do.

We urge the delegation of the Western North Carolina Conference to support the Modified Traditional Plan in the upcoming General Conference.

We love The United Methodist Church and long for the day when it is comprehensively surrendered to the beauty of God's design for sexuality.

Remember the math:

## Low Anxiety + High Clarity = Zero Fallout

While we're on the subject of *Honest Declarations*, it's time to set another myth to rest: "The young people will leave us." Change what the church teaches about sex, the thinking goes, or you will lose a generation of young people raised in a sexualized and sexually tolerant culture. The overwhelming presence of young adults in modern, non-denominational megachurches who hold to an ancient sexual ethic suggests otherwise. As to the intriguing words of a new voice in the Methodist Twitterverse: *UMC Young And Orthodox.* Here is the take:

> There's a widely-accepted lie that all young United Methodists are theologically progressive, but that's simply not the case. While it's true that many, perhaps most, are, it's also true that those of us who are both young and theologically orthodox are often afraid to speak up.

> I can't speak for everyone, but I can speak for myself. In seminary, I saw constant praise for innovative, novel ideas that challenged the historical teachings of the Church. I'm not just talking about LGBTQIA+ topics, but even things as fundamental as Jesus' divinity/humanity.

> Anything traditional had to be justified and defended at a much higher standard. This can be helpful in some ways, because it forces you to be able to articulate your beliefs, but it's disingenuous to pretend it doesn't also reveal an endorsement of heterodoxy.

> The seminary culture I experienced was also profoundly

negative. To hear the things my peers said about those who disagreed with them was crushing, because it was merciless and cruel. There's no assumption of good intent, no consideration that you could disagree without hatred.

Ostensibly, the "Young People's Statement" recognized disagreement while calling for unity, but really a part of UMC Discipleship Ministries endorsed changing church policy in the name of "young people." There was no similar petition published for the Traditional Plan.

Traditional or orthodox young people, especially clergy, are in a position now where believing in long-established standards can lead to being ostracized by their peers and having their motives and faith questioned, and where their denomination is failing to give them a platform.

All that to say, I felt it was important to provide a different perspective to some of the conversations I see. As I said before, this is certainly not just about human sexuality, but is rather about bringing a young, orthodox voice to this space.[3]

It turns out the *"UMC, Young & Orthodox"* is not oxymoronic; more likely, it is an underserved population speaking with high clarity and serving within our midst.

This simply serves as my plea for all of us in the United Methodist family to replace the frustration of Holy Conversation with the liberation of Honest Declaration. Even in the United States, we might find ourselves surprised with where the honesty leads us.

### 3. Negotiated Release Instead Of Tortured Repeat?

I was not present in St. Louis, as I was a barely-elected reserve delegate and opted to take a mission trip to India instead. Nevertheless, from colleagues and friends who attended GC '19, the song remains the same: please don't put us through that again. Instead of the Zero-Sum Game of a Business-As-Usual General Conference 2020, where even victory feels like defeat, I believe our destination is a place of mutual release. I am personally pleased that the Global Coalition can enter these negotiations from a place of strength and conviction, from which we can offer grace and renewal. But at this

[3] @YoungMethodist., March 23, 2019. https://twitter.com/YoungMethodist

stage, minds are not changing, hearts are not softening, and there are no new compromises to be invented. United Methodism has decided who it is once again. How we peacefully multiply in a way that honors both our declared identity and our global connection is our next great task.

**Talbot Davis** was born and raised in Dallas, Texas. After graduating from high school in 1980, he attended Princeton University in Princeton, NJ, where he played varsity tennis for four years, served as team captain, and graduated with honors in English in 1984.

Talbot is a 1990 graduate of Asbury Theological Seminary in Wilmore, KY. In 28 years of full-time United Methodist ministry in the Western North Carolina Annual Conference, he has served two appointments: Mt. Carmel-Midway (1990-1999) and Good Shepherd (1999-present).

Talbot's preaching and teaching ministry caught the eye of Abingdon Press which has turned five of his sermon series into books: *Head Scratchers, The Storm Before The Calm, The Shadow Of A Doubt, Solve, and Crash Test Dummies: Surprising Lessons From The Book Of Judges.*

Photo by Kevin Slimp, Market Square Books

For weeks prior to General Conference, Rev. Wil Cantrell visited churches to explain the various proposals being discussed by delegates.

# CHAPTER NINE
# Katie Z. Dawson
Maybe We Need a Pentecost Moment

"My feet are strong, my eyes are clear / I cannot see the way from here..."

With those words, Sandra McCracken opens her song "God's Highway." In an interview with Song Story, she talks about in times of great uncertainty and unknowing, sometimes we need to sing our way forward.[1] We need to sing into being the strength and clarity that we desire.

I must admit that trying to answer the question of where we are and where we go from here feels almost impossible. It feels like we are fundamentally broken. There is a brokenness in a polity that discerns God's will with a majority vote in a legislative process. There is a brokenness in a global church that values the contextualization of ministry in some places, but not in all. There is a brokenness in the very Body of Christ, specifically in our conditional acceptance of LGBTQIA+ siblings.

I feel like I have been swimming in a fog of grief since the special called General Conference and every time I have sat down to think about what comes next, the words fail me. It is as if the church that baptized and confirmed me, helped me to hear God's call in my life, the church I have faithfully served for more than twelve years, died on Tuesday, the 26th of February. And the way we have all splintered and run away to our separate corners feels a lot like the aftermath of Good Friday. The disciples have scattered and The United Methodist Church has been buried in a tomb of legislative action.

Maybe I need to draw upon the strength of McCracken's lyrics and write my way forward.

---

[1] McCracken, Sandra, "Sandra McCracken – God's Highway", YouTube video, Interview by Song Story, published August 31, 2016, https://www.youtube.com/watch?v=YnouUQQgEdE.

## Broken Pews, Broken Polity

Last summer, my local church determined that the fifty-year-old pews in our sanctuary needed to be replaced. When our sanctuary was built, the same year as the formation of The United Methodist Church, the pews were the last item to be completed. The budget had run low and so the church chose a less expense laminate wood for the seating.

For the last ten to fifteen years, that laminate has been chipping away. Here and there we are able to repair and patch, but the pews have noticeable wear. Not only that, but the seating itself began to be unstable in some places. More than a couple of times, a support has given way, only to be shored up by skilled volunteers in the church. We sought the advice of a company on whether our pews could be rehabilitated and the answer that came back was that it would be less expensive to simply replace them.

The church today is different in many ways from the church of fifty years ago. We like to think we are more nimble, modern, and flexible. Some wanted us to make a change and install pew chairs instead of the permanently placed pews of the past. Others wanted to cling to the tradition and the look of what had been. Lines were drawn in the sand and one couple even threatened to leave if we purchased chairs and not pews.

I tell this story only because as the pastor of this congregation, I could see the conflict stirring up and knew that this couldn't simply be a decision we took by a majority vote. We sought the input of the whole congregation in the process and focused less on a hard-and-fast either/or of pews and chairs, and instead invited people to lift up the values they wanted to prioritize. Traditional or Modern? Simple or Ornate? Flexible or Permanent? Comfort or Stability? Our leadership spent many months in conversation listening to church members. We presented the variety of options before us in as many different venues as possible. Only then did we turn to a vote and ended up with a unanimous decision that allowed for compromise in our space with both pews and pew chairs, in a similar style.

If I had a sense as their pastor that the vote would have been less than a super majority, I never would have brought it to a vote. It would have meant that we were not yet ready to decide. We would have needed to spend more time in relationship and in exploring creative options we had not yet discovered. After all, we were going to be making an expensive decision that this congregation would have to support and live with for many generations to come. When

70

you walk into our sanctuary today, it truly has been transformed by the new seating, adding an openness and brightness that we didn't realize we needed.

I had such hope in the work of the Commission on a Way Forward because they were brought together outside of our typical legislative structure. I saw in the effort the pastoral leadership I tried to embody in my own congregation. I believed that the time they spent together in a conciliar process would truly allow for holy conferencing and consensus building. The Commission had the freedom of time to build relationship, test ideas, compromise, and struggle together. And yet, even that time together could not produce a singular vision of where God was leading us into the future. Even if they had, my fear was that as soon as the process was out of their hands, our structure would do what our structure does best: turn it into a legislative battle. With a multiplicity of directions on the table, we did just that.

> *"Whatever decisions we did or didn't make in St. Louis were going to leave a permanent mark on our church."*

Whatever decisions we did or didn't make in St. Louis were going to leave a permanent mark on our church. We are trapped within a legislative process that creates winners and losers. Out of the hands of the Commission, the lines in the sand became clear. I was a reserve delegate in Tampa in 2012 and was seated in Portland in 2016. Unlike those experiences, the rhetoric, spin, and lobbying going into our 2019 gathering were divisive and ugly. In the final weeks before St. Louis, I came to dread opening my mail, unsure of gross mischaracterizations of people, scripture, and the legislation itself I would discover. Once we arrived, our legislative actions, speeches, and process were damaging to the witness of Jesus Christ in this world.

How desperately I wanted someone to call a time-out so that we could step back from the brink and take a deep breath. General Conference is the only body that has the authority to speak for The United Methodist Church. However, the truth is, we are entrenched in a conflict that cannot be legislated away. A body that speaks as only fifty-three percent of the whole has no real witness in the world.

What would it look like for our church to be conciliar instead of legislative? What would it look like for our denomination to use a circle process of holy conferencing instead of Robert's Rules? What would it look like if all of our decisions needed to have a consensus of at least a super-majority before passing?

## A Broken Global Connection

In April of 2019, we celebrated two hundred years of mission as a church. At the event, "Answering the Call," we lifted the legacy of missionaries, deaconesses, doctors, churches, and ordinary people who have crossed boundaries and borders to share the love of God with the world. We also named and confessed that sometimes in the attempt to do the right thing, we caused harm, hurt, and imposed ideas upon others. One presentation noted how the introduction of the plow into South Rhodesia was an attempt to lessen the burden upon women who cultivated with hoes. Yet, when the men took their place behind those plows, they discovered they no longer needed four wives and dismissed the secondary wives and children back to their families. A move to empower women ended up destroying their place in that culture.

I serve as a Director with the General Board of Global Ministries. I have been so grateful during these last few years to learn about the ways that we are owning the mistakes we have made in the past and seeking mutuality in our missional relationships. The slogan "From Everywhere to Everywhere" is based on a deep theological understanding of the incarnational presence of God wherever we are in mission. It is not that *we* have something to offer *those* people, but that God is already at work and we are invited to join in the *Missio Dei*. Our missionaries are now coming from all over the world and the cross-cultural learning and exchange is enriching and revitalizing our church!

One of my first real entry points to global mission was through the work of "Imagine No Malaria." I was invited to serve as the Iowa Conference Field Coordinator for the fundraising efforts in our state. What I witnessed in the work of "Imagine No Malaria" was The United Methodist Church as a global and connected church. Locally in Iowa, congregations joined together for pancake suppers and lemonade stands. We didn't have the terminology of "progressive" and "traditionalist" back then, but no matter your theological stance, everyone young and old could get behind the vision of a world where children were not dying from a preventable disease. It empowered and gave life to our local churches and was also a positive witness to our larger community about the impact of faith in the world.

It also gave us a window into what it meant to be a global church. I must admit, our work was sometimes tinged with that legacy of paternalism as we raised funds to send to some faraway place to make their lives better. Early on in our training as field coordinators, we discovered how the good intentions of our previous work of "Nothing But Nets" was flawed because it often dropped hundreds and thousands of free nets into a community without an infrastructure of support or a true conversation with the communities about what their needs and experiences were.

"Imagine No Malaria" was not simply a re-branding effort. It sought to learn from those experiences and redirected the focus towards building up community health networks and empowering local leadership, revitalizing infrastructure, and listening to what each unique context needed in its work to prevent malaria. We focused on the connections between malaria, water, sanitation projects, and the dire need for the health system to be strengthened. We began purchasing nets in-country instead of disrupting local economies with outside products. Our efforts, along with global partners, have helped to cut in half the mortality rate for malaria! And, the reality is, there are still critiques to be made about blind spots in those efforts.

These experiences have drastically impacted the lens upon which I see our global connection. There is immense power in the reality that our cross and flame is a symbol of hope, health, and abundant life in this world. We have a seat at the table with powerful international players because of our credibility and competency in disaster response, human services, and peacemaking work. The relationships developed between conferences, like the 20+ years of the Iowa-Nigeria Partnership, have transformed lives in both places. The United States now needs that witness of hope, perseverance, and faithfulness from our siblings across the world as we find ourselves in post-Christian decline.

We are imperfect people living in an imperfect structure. Our global structure and polity were designed, in part, to protect central conferences from colonialization and an imposition of Western values through the ability to adapt the *Book of Discipline* for their contexts. This made sense when the power dynamics were weighted heavily in favor of the U.S. leadership. However, as those numbers have shifted, and the demographic center of the church has shifted, the polity has not.

Now, our entire body participates in votes that impact only half of the connection. The disparity in our economic relationships are also significant. Even partnerships like the one between Iowa and Nigeria must be adjusted so there is mutuality, rather than a model of toxic charity. Even when we try to have conscientious conversations about these realities, the vestiges of colonialism, racism, classism, and privilege seep into our work.

What if our theology and ecclesiology was fully contextualized in each and every cultural soil? What if our polity was not based on finances or structure, but on relationship? What if we decoupled our theology and mission from Western dominance and rediscovered indigenous and ethnic cultural identities? What if our General Conference was a place where we could gather to discuss, learn, and celebrate how God is making disciples and transforming the world?

## A Broken Body of Christ

I supported the One Church Plan and the Simple Plan because I deeply value our connection with one another as the body of Christ. None of us can say to another, "I have no need of you" (1 Corinthians 12:12-26, NRSV). This is true even when we disagree or find the actions of others within our midst to be discriminatory. In fact, those disagreements and conflicts highlight the importance of community, accountability, humility, and love. If we truly believe the actions or beliefs of another person in our body are harmful or inaccurate, we cannot work towards transformation, redemption, or repentance if we remove, expel, or walk away from one another.

I also believe that LGBTQIA+ persons are vital to the life of our church and are called by God into relationship and ministry. I have experienced the faithful witness of my LGBTQIA+ siblings and I cannot deny the way the Holy Spirit has called them to serve our church, as lay and clergy, single and married. The United Methodist Church suffers when it rejects the ministry and witness of those among us who consistently demonstrate incarnational love and challenge the binaries that so often divide this world.

Some parts of this body are suffering because of their conditional acceptance. One recent study in *The American Journal of Preventative Medicine* shows that queer youth are significantly more likely to have suicidal thoughts than straight peers. More troubling, those for whom religion is important were thirty-eight percent more likely to have suicidal thoughts than non-religious queer peers.[2] When we tell our precious children that they are of sacred worth but a fundamental part of their identity makes them incompatible with our tradition, we are causing immense harm.

I struggle with the tension between a longing for a "big tent" United Methodism that would allow us to continue to be in ministry together and the real harm that we cause to LGBTQIA+ persons through our policies. I clearly hear from my queer siblings that a

---

[2] https://www.huffpost.com/entry/queer-youth-religion-suicide-study_n_5ad4f7b3e4b-077c89ceb9774_

unity built on exclusion and discrimination is false and unholy, but so is a compromise that allows for continued discrimination in parts of the connection. What is our witness to children growing up in more traditional parts of our church? How will compromise impact LGBTQIA+ members of our church in those places globally where homosexuality is illegal or punishable by death. How do we balance the call for full inclusion with the reality that a broken and divided church will limit our ability to speak for the sacred worth of all persons in those places, too?

I believed the church could be a witness to how people can disagree in love. I worked for a church where progressives and traditionalists could be honest about their differences, practice according to their conscience, and hold one another accountable for the places we each get it wrong. I saw in our *Book of Discipline* a vision of church where contextual ministry is valued and thoughtful theological reflection is encouraged. I also valued a denomination willing to continue working towards perfection by amending and adapting our shared covenant every four years.

I hoped we could values connection and diversity by living into that old maxim, "in essentials, unity; in non-essentials, liberty; and in all things, charity."[3] I want to be clear that I didn't think human sexuality is an non-essential part of our identity, or that systemic discrimination is a non-essential problem of sin in the body of Christ. Rather, I believed that "essentials" pointed to the core doctrinal statements of our Christian faith like the Trinity and the resurrection of Christ and the primacy of scripture.

In addition, I saw it as an invitation to show one another grace, freedom, and love. United Methodists disagree about how to interpret six verses of scripture historically understood to condemn homosexuality in the Bible (Genesis 19:4- 5; Leviticus 18:22, 20:13; Romans 1:29-31; 1 Corinthians 6:9-10, and 1 Timothy 1:9-10). I think my more conservative siblings are wrong and they think I am wrong, but we each start with the centrality of scripture. In relationship, in dialogue and conversation, by wrestling together, we glimpse God's truth. The witness of scripture itself is that any one claim to the good news of God is not enough (i.e.: we have four gospels, not one) and that the church has always wrestled on matters of tradition and interpretation (see Acts 15). Our official doctrine of The United Methodist Church, the Articles of Religion of the Methodist Church, even leaves room for discretion and contextuality on matters of marriage and religious ceremonies (Article XXI and XXII).

---

[3] http://www.umc.org/what-we-believe/section-2-our-doctrinal-history

The thrust of the Traditional Plan was to take one theological interpretation of how to contextually practice ministry and enshrine it as doctrine. We have declared that there is only one way of being a faithful United Methodist. Language included in the original petitions, but which didn't make it to the floor for a final vote, encouraged people who cannot uphold this particular interpretation to leave the denomination: either as individuals, churches, or as whole annual conferences. The rationale for the "Implementing Gracious Accountability" petition called it "the heart of the Traditional Plan." Unity in The United Methodist Church is now a forced uniformity that homosexuality is incompatible with Christian teaching.

Not all the pieces of the plan were voted on, or were constitutional. However, pieces that remain will push centrists and progressives committed to inclusion out of leadership, through mandatory penalties and limits on whom can be affirmed for ministry. Also, one petition says self-avowed homosexuals cannot be licensed, commissioned, or ordained. Note, the final legislation DID NOT include the word "practicing." Amendments would have fixed this inadvertent mistake, but were not added.

I feel as if the General Conference rejected everything I believed to be true about what it means to be church together. But my grief and pain is dwarfed by the harm we have done to the witness of the gospel and to the lives of our LGBTQIA+ siblings. Many of our LGBTQIA+ members and their families feel like they have just been rejected by the church. I can no longer sit back and remain neutral when it comes to the lives and ministry of my LGBTQIA+ siblings. I also recognize that I have a lot of hard work and repentance to do around what it means to truly be an ally.

As I shared with my congregation on the Sunday after General Conference, these next few years are going to be ugly and messy. We did everything within our power to keep from dividing the denomination during those four days in St. Louis. In those four days, however, we exposed the rift and I believe efforts will be made at the next 2020 General Conference to strategically and carefully formalize that divide.

Providentially, the season of Lent began just as our grief set in. My first message to my theologically divided congregation was to wait. I knew that some were already expressing their desire to throw in the towel and leave. Others expressed their relief, but also frustration, at the turmoil of their fellow members. Some told me they were embarrassed by what our denomination now represents.

Acting out of grief is never a good idea, so I invited my congregation to journey through Lent with me. I called them to rest in the presence of God and the community of this church. After all, our relationships with one another were not severed by the vote of 438 people. There is still time to reach out to people with whom we disagree and share a cup of coffee. We were still called to care for one another in love.

Over the weeks of Lent, we did just that. We collected funds to send feminine hygiene products to our neighbors on the Missouri River who were flooded. We made over two hundred bags out of donated t-shirts for a local homeless shelter. We finished up a sixty-one-day chronological study of scripture. We launched a new Covenant Discipleship Group that will multiply into three new groups this summer. And, we hosted our first "family conversation" at the church where over one-third of our regular attenders showed up to ask questions and describe the kind of church they were longing for in the future. There is still tension and disagreement in our midst, but at least we are talking with one another in a real and honest way. That is what the body of Christ does.

What comes next? Does the body shatter into a million pieces? Do we slowly dissolve and die? Can or should the United Methodist Church even be saved? When I reflect on our structural sins like colonialism, homophobia, and sexism, there are days I'm tempted to simply leave the church behind like so many peers my age have done.

Or maybe we resist. Since the General Conference rejected the idea of compromise and contextuality, people are turning away from the center and finding their voices. Petitions, letters, and ads in newspapers are popping up throughout the connection. Alongside the commitments to full inclusion, my colleagues and I are also willing to begin the hard work of repentance for the harm we have caused by prioritizing the institution over the lives of our siblings.

Maybe there is still time for resurrection. As time has passed, I feel less like we are in a hopeless place of grieving and more like we are living in those days right after Easter. Like the disciples, holed up together in Jerusalem, we have caught a glimpse of resurrection and hear rumors of life, but have our doubts. We are seeing, touching, and naming the wounds that were inflicted upon the body, but have not yet discovered how it has changed the church or what it means to live again. It is comforting to remember it took fifty days before the disciples shook off their confusion and stupor before the Holy Spirit filled them with the ability to lead in a new direction.

What if we all acknowledged our privileges, listening to and prioritizing voices that are marginalized so we can be a part of what God is doing? What if we learned from our queer siblings that God has been enfleshed among us and took the time to develop and promote a healthy theology of the body and sexuality? What if this body came together with one voice to affirm the sacred worth of all persons and to actively fight against policies in nations across our connection that criminalize homosexuality?

What we need right now is a Pentecost moment. During one of the evenings of General Conference, folks gathered in a hotel basement to strategize for the next day. It was a diverse coalition of centrists and progressives, and to be honest, it was a difficult experience. I came out of that room realizing we have a lot of work to do if we want to do this thing called "church" together. We need to overcome the racism, sexism, homophobia, classism, and clericalism of our past and present relationships.

If what comes next for the UMC is a resurrected church led by imperfect people from all over the world, we are going to need the Holy Spirit to show up and help us understand each other.

**Rev. Katie Z. Dawson** is an ordained elder serving as the lead pastor at Immanuel UMC in Des Moines, Iowa. She is also active in our connectional church as a Director with the General Board of Global Ministries. She studied communications, religion, and physics at Simpson College and received her Master of Divinity from Vanderbilt University Divinity School. Katie and her husband, Brandon enjoy hosting a weekly board game night at their house. She is the author of three books, "Three Gifts, One Christ," "The Lord Is Our Salvation," and "All Earth is Waiting." When she can find time, Katie blogs at www.salvagedfaith.com

# CHAPTER TEN
# Bishop Bob Farr
A Methodist Dumpster Fire

When I served as a volunteer fire chief, one of the alarms I dreaded responding to was for a dumpster fire. It's smelly, it's messy, and it can be dangerous. Dumpster fires are notoriously difficult to extinguish. It's never over when you think it's over because materials thrown into dumpsters tend to smolder and are notoriously hard to put out. Inexperienced fire fighters might dump water on it and walk away only to have it ignite minutes or even hours later. Experienced fire professionals don't take dumpster fires lightly. They can be just as dangerous as a structural fire and often involve hazardous materials that people have carelessly thrown into the trash. One memorable dumpster fire included a propane tank explosion immediately before my team arrived on site.

The thing about dumpster fires is that in order to extinguish one, you must spread all the burning material out on the ground and let it sit there for a while. Getting it all out in the open is helpful in seeing what you're truly dealing with before you begin to resolve it.

My experience of General Conference reminded me a bit of a dumpster fire. We are not quite sure what the future holds because we are still determining what materials are smoldering. What qualifies as a dumpster fire in the church depends on who's watching, but you tend know it when you see it. If forced to define it for someone not prone to social media, you might quote Merriam-Webster:

> **Dumpster fire** (noun, U.S. informal): *"an utterly calamitous or mismanaged situation or occurrence: disaster."*

It might be easy to identify the 2019 Special Session of General Conference as a dumpster fire of sorts. I don't think this analogy completely fits, but I think it's a helpful way of understanding what happened and how to move forward. We have had a very public fight among our United Methodist family, and before we may be tempted to dump a bunch of water on it and walk away, we might take a page from fire service professionals and allow the smoldering remains of this painful public conversation to lay on the ground before we try to extinguish it. I realize this waiting is a painful time for many in our connection who have been waiting for over forty years or more. My bent toward putting out the fire and removing the remnants of the disaster may not be what is needed right now. Our need to immediately rescue the situation may not be what is needed. We may just need to sit with it awhile.

Might we learn from the friends of Job that advice-giving and lecturing might not be what is needed? His three friends, Elihaz, Bildad, and Zophar attempted to console him by giving him a tongue-lashing, advising him to repent, and to seek God's mercy. Yet, Job needed to sit with his suffering for a while. A disaster has befallen us as a group. Our hurts and pains are all laid out on the table before us. Perhaps our best next step is to sit with the pain, particularly, the pain of those directly affected by the decisions of the Special Session, the LGBTQIA+ community and their allies.

When I was invited to share my thoughts on where we are as a church and where we go from here, I hesitated because I do not want to be like Job's friends, who did not know how to be good friends and grieve with their suffering brother. I worry that any "answer" I might share to the questions of "where we are as a church and where we are headed?" will be reactionary rather than responsive. Even as I submit my chapter, we await the Judicial Council's response to the declaratory decision. As always, I include my caveats and reminders that I am not an academic.

The broad range of writers sharing in this volume will certainly offer an example or two of deeply intelligent and systematic approaches to the impact on our ecclesiology. Others will share missiological essays. My humble offering, on the other hand, will be more a pragmatic approach. I'm a local church guy who has spent a ministerial career trying to connect new people with Jesus Christ. This is the lens that continues to shape my work as a bishop in The United Methodist Church.

As with any pragmatist, there is a certain amount of inconsistency in my approach to ministry because I prize the local context above all others. When one does this, it often means that "one-size fits-all" approaches do not work. Situational leadership means that decisions cannot be uniform. I learned a lot of this as a parent to two very different children. Susan and I did not parent them the same way. The ways in which we encouraged good behavior and disciplined poor decisions were different based on each child. That has also been my experience in the local church. My missional context as a pastor in urban Kansas City was very different from my experience as a student pastor in rural Texas or as a senior pastor in a large established church in suburban St. Charles County. I had to adapt and shift in order to connect with the mission field. What worked in one place did not always work in another. The certainty around some things I thought I'd never do in ministry dissolved as I realized that I needed to change our approach in order to connect the Gospel with new people.

*The thing about dumpster fires is that in order to extinguish one, you must spread all the burning material out on the ground and let it sit there for a while.*

As a local pastor, I often bristled at anything that created more obstacles for the local church to do ministry in its context. I wanted the support of my bishop and conference while offering me the freedom to serve my people in the best way I could. As a bishop, I continue to prioritize the local church over everything else, and I am still resistant to the General Church creating uniform practices or procedures that would handcuff local church pastors from serving their missional context. We should be unleashing our ministerial leaders to the world rather than restricting their ability to serve new generations.

Using the language made popular by Tom Lamprecht and Tom Berlin's teaching over the past two years, I am best described as a traditional-compatibilist. I can live within (and oversee) a conference that offers an openness to same-sex marriage. As a traditionalist, however, I continue to struggle with the ordination of LGBTQIA+ persons. I realize the contradictions in my ecclesiology, but I am torn. In my continued learning on this topic, I have found myself convicted both by a biblical reading for inclusion as well as a scriptural reading that affirms a more traditional understanding of sexual behavior. I simply want to locate my shifting and sometimes inconsistent tension on this topic as I confess that aspects of inclusion challenge me personally and would force me to serve beyond my comfort zone. On the other hand, I have always placed a high value on people's competencies above all else. I know there are highly competent and gifted people in the LGBTQIA+ community who are called by God to vocational ministry. Right now, I just am not sure how to make that work in my context.

The fact is, whether I am comfortable with it or not, I am already living with this reality. If I were a hard-core traditionalist, I would have already investigated clergy who I suspect are at present performing same-sex weddings or questioned gay clergy on whether they are celibate. I have not and I have no interest in doing so. Furthermore, I have not fully examined anyone who I believe is not in full compliance with the *Book of Discipline* on any number of other issues. All of us have fallen short of the standards of the *Book of Discipline*. I doubt I would have any pastors left if forced to investigate whether all clergy were following it to the letter.

## Everything has Shifted

The Special Session of General Conference was a gut-wrenching experience full of sadness for my beloved church in which I was born, baptized, confirmed, called, ordained, and have served for 41 years and been consecrated as bishop. While I was not surprised by the outcome, I was shocked and disappointed by the coarseness of our debate and the bitterness of our fight. I am so sorry for all the hurt our publicized debate has caused and the ways in which our decisions continue to harm.

I was not surprised the One Church model did not pass. I have said from the beginning that it was not passable. I was not surprised the Traditional Plan passed. The fact is many people in our church wanted the Traditional Plan and that plan works for a significant part of the global church. However, there is a part of our church for which this plan does not work, and it does not work for a number of our pastors and churches in Missouri.

I was against the Traditional Plan because it understood "united" as uniformity of thought and practice and didn't allow for contextuality. As I have previously stated, this rubs against my pragmatic and contextualized understanding of local church ministry. This is so far away from the Methodism in which I grew up.

My first pastor was the Rev. Marie Hyatt, the first ordained woman clergyperson in the Missouri West Conference. She taught me about the "big tent" that Methodism offered. It was in that little church in Creighton, Missouri that I discovered Democrats and Republicans worshipped together, business leaders and farmers sat side by side, and women and men shared leadership within the community (with women probably shouldering more than their fair share). It appears that in our global dynamic, this type of contextualized ministry and "big tent" underpinning is no longer fully appreciated.

I share Candler School of Theology Dean Jan Love's opinion stated in her February 26, 2019 issue of *Candler News & Events*, that said:

*I have also asserted, however that shared church governance structures across radically different cultural traditions are a really bad idea. Churches from the Wesleyan tradition make decisions about their shared life together very differently depending on whether they come from the Philippines, Germany, the Congo, Liberia, Mozambique, Russia or any other country. Moreover, from my point of view, the power disparities between churches in rich and poor countries are so stark that we risk reproducing new forms of colonialism when we naively seek to govern ourselves under one set of rules that reflect on Western cultural traditions.*

*My worst fears about the hazards of formal shared church governance across vastly different cultural differences, even with the best of intentions, have come true in this Special Session of the General Conference.*

In 1968, The United Methodist Church was born out of religious pluralism and structured with a 19th century framework that could not possibly imagine the radically different theological directions and socio-economic demands that would inhabit the church's life in the 21st century. The United Methodist Church was meant to hold many differences together, but not unlimited differences, much less, irreconcilable differences. Creating a structure that requires uniformity across radically different contexts is a poor and outdated idea. It does not honor the global diversity of the Church, nor does it anticipate the power of the Holy Spirit to spring forth and make ways in the wilderness and bring water to dry ground.

## Divergence

The plan I favored, the Connectional Conference Plan (CCP), didn't seem to have much hope in passing due to its complexity, but I ultimately think it had the most adaptability and the most promise for the future due to the following reasons:

- It downsizes and restructures the General Church for better missional service, something I have longed for most of my career.

- It allows persons and churches to follow their convictions and reside within a shared-values system.

- It is more adaptive, creative, and provides space to conferences and local churches for missional contextualization.

- It offers a new understanding of unity and polity for a global denomination without sacrificing local and regional needs.

- It allows for a potential reunification in the future.

> *"Here's the rub. The General Conference asked the Council to lead and yet they did not agree with the recommenda- tion of a majority of the bishops."*

Despite its lack of a public hearing at General Conference, I anticipate that we might find ourselves in the CCP by default. The real question will be whether we go there in an orderly fashion by our own accord or by sheer chaos as individuals and groups of individuals splinter and fracture.

While we have spent much time wringing our hands around unity or the lack thereof, a schism of sorts has occurred whether we wanted it or not. A 53 percent approval of the petitions associated with the "Traditional PLan" is not a clear mandate on how to move forward. It's time to recognize that The United Methodist Church is practicing as (at least) two separate denominations. If we weren't legally bound by the same polity, we could probably get along just fine around missional work like UMCOR and Global Ministries and our shared commitments to our personnel through Wespath's work.

It is time to find a way for The United Methodist Church to separate so we can stop harming one another and return to the main work of the church: sharing the transforming power and grace of Jesus Christ. There is no point in going further when, quite simply, there is no scenario in which anyone wins. There is no point in trying to force the other side to do what it cannot stomach. While we fight, we risk losing the next generation no matter what side we are on in this death match. Nobody wants to join a church that is waging an internal war with itself.

We have all lost friends and been wounded in this battle. I am a passionate leader, but I'm not passionate about this fight over sexuality. I'm passionate about proclaiming Christ. I'm passionate about the Wesleyan Way. I'm passionate about transforming people, churches, and communities for Christ. I'm passionate about the growth of the church. I'm passionate about becoming a younger, more diverse, more relevant movement for Jesus Christ. Nothing much changed in St. Louis related to our existing disciplinary standards. Yet, our irreconcilable differences became very public and everything shifted. I don't believe the fight is worth the cost of the future and further harm to one another.

## Where does leadership come from?

There has always been a healthy suspicion of the episcopacy within the Methodist movement. This isn't new. My Missouri colleague and United Methodist polity expert, Dr. Tom Frank, has spent a great deal of time researching the office of bishop and the constraints, concerns, and possibilities for episcopal leadership. He is far better equipped at sharing the challenges to the episcopacy through our history and should be consulted as we consider navigating our way forward related to polity changes. And yet, as they say, all politics is local. We are skeptical of the Council of Bishops but for the most part, people trust their resident bishop. We look to localized leaders to lead through difficult times.

But, here's the rub. The General Conference asked the Council to lead and yet they did not agree with the recommendation of a majority of the bishops in their support of the One Church Plan. Perhaps in an ironic move, the General Conference rejected the plan that pushed power away from the episcopacy toward conferences, churches, and clergy and instead, passed the plan that secured authority with resident bishops to enforce disciplinary requirements.

Most bishops said they didn't want the power to enforce disciplinary standards on sexuality, and yet with one vote, the General Conference secured that enforcement would reside within the episcopal office. It's contradictory, confusing, and hard to imagine what this might mean for our future, but as with any time of crisis, localized leadership will play a critical role in guiding the Church forward.

## Navigating a Way Forward

The constitution of The United Methodist Church identifies the annual conference as "the basic body in the Church." The annual conference admits persons into ordained ministry, and it is from the annual conference that clergy are appointed to their assignments. Clergy hold their membership in the annual conference and not in congregations.

I believe, for the next season, The United Methodist Church will function in a diocesan model. In other words, bishops will manage their conferences as they see fit, as many already practice. Some bishops will follow the directives of the General Conference, some will defy the directives, and some will try to manage a middle way through the chaos. The fact that no bishop has resigned as a matter of principle over the whole issue should be a sign that we have all compromised our principles at some point or another. We are all running our individual conferences as if we were in a diocesan model already.

We may look to the Acts church as a guide for a new understanding of unity. When Paul and Barnabas divided up the mission field in a newly formed Jewish-Christianity, they understood it as a *division of labor, not a division of mission*. It was a new way to understand unity. The United Methodist Church might also understand our way forward in this same approach. By returning to the bedrock of Methodism, with the annual conference as the primary unit, and committing to one another that our differences on this issue amount to a division of labor and not of mission, we may have a future that allows for true contextualized ministry that glorifies God.

In 2020, we might call a constitutional convention to allow for the creation of a new constitution. Within this setting, we might jettison jurisdictional, central, and annual conferences and convert all conferences into affiliated autonomous conferences that come together every four years for worship, learning, and mission. If churches disagreed with the direction of the annual conference, there would be a pathway for local churches to switch annual conferences with a time window for that transfer to occur. Since clergy membership remains with the annual conference, there would always be a pathway for clergy to transfer to different annual conferences. Concordat agreements among the annual conferences would mean that we could accept each other's ordination and share in ministry together in a similar way to our existing full communion relationships.

I would set free the general agencies to become resource agencies rather than regulatory ones. They are already incorporated, governed by a board, hire their own general secretaries, and have their own investments, endowments, and reserves. They are already structured for this to happen. It would allow for the agencies to be freed for good work in their area of focus and provide them additional avenues for revenue rather than apportionment dependency. I am not opposed to utilizing general agencies. In Missouri, we use agency resources when they are excellent and when they help our local churches fulfill the mission of the church. We are past the age where we need regulatory agencies to tell annual conferences how to do their local business.

The episcopacy would have to be restructured and annual conferences would have to determine their terms and conditions for episcopal leadership. The annual conference through the Board of Ordained Ministry would still decide who gets to be ordained and licensed, and appointive powers would continue to reside with resident bishops. This would require annual conferences to make localized decisions about things like same-sex marriage and ordination, but it would be an annual conference decision, not a local church one. Conferences are better equipped to guide their conference into the future. I realize that for some progressive incompatibilists, this change will not be quick enough and for traditional incompatibilists, it will be too swift a change, but I do think autonomous conferences could step their way toward inclusion with this approach at a pace that fits their context.

If given the opportunity to become its own autonomous conference, I'm not sure what Missouri will do. It is possible we would allow pastors to have the opportunity to preside over same-sex marriages. Ordination of self-avowed, practicing homosexuals may come in time as the conference decides. I believe it's easier for annual conferences to make this walk into the future with people they know rather than fighting at General Conference where we don't know each other, lose our individual voices, and we are relegated into voting "yes" or "no" which leads to clear winners and losers. We Methodists don't leap well, but I believe a conference is in a better position to take the appropriate steps forward that fit their context. And I would encourage my Missouri Conference to take steps into inclusion rather than leaps. It is a conference decision about who shall be our pastors. I am a proponent that most decisions need to be made at the annual conference level to allow for the most contextualized ministry possible. The days of top-down decision-making are gone.

In the early days of Methodism, the annual conference was the foundational element of our movement, and our current constitution still states that the annual conference is the "fundamental body of the church" (2016 *Book of Discipline* – Article IV ¶11). With a focus on the annual conference and concordat agreements among those conferences, I think we would see fruit-bearing across the entirety of the church. And, like Paul and Barnabas, we will be equipped to share our witness more broadly with the world in different ways and alleviate our 40-year fight. Paul warns, "But if you are always biting and devouring one another, watch out! Beware of destroying one another" (Galatians 5:15, NLT).

## Conclusion

In a dumpster fire, after it's sorted, you put all the fire remnants back into the dumpster and move on, allowing the sanitation crew to do their work. I am not convinced that's the right move for the church. We cannot put it out of sight any longer. In fact, it seems to me that our church has been way overdue for this conversation. Our inability to speak generously and appropriately about sexuality is partially due to our lack of experience in conversing about it. As we try to navigate and lead forward, I think we need to explore how best to fulfill our ultimate mission of making disciples of Jesus Christ for the transformation of the world. We have learned we cannot do that by trying to change people's convictions about scriptural interpretation. We need a process that will allow people to identify their values and follow their convictions. This will likely mean going to separate models of Methodism.

Exploring a way forward loosely together requires a different understanding of unity. Unity does not necessarily mean uniformity. Paul and Barnabas learned that in time. It is taking us a while to learn that lesson as well. Jesus desired unity in mission, praying that we may be as one just as he and the Father were one "so that the world will believe you sent me" (John 17:21, NLT). We can be unified around mission, have different ways of interpreting scripture, as well as different ways of structuring ourselves for the work and ministry of the church, and still be true to Christ's prayer that we be as one. This method of doing ministry in the name of Christ is as old as the beginnings of our faith.

We know that uniformity is not a distinguishing characteristic of The United Methodist Church. If all my churches were uniform, it would not take as much time, resources, and talent (nine district superintendents in the case of Missouri) to figure out what pastor should go where. We would just draw names out of a hat because all the churches would be alike. Therefore, any pastor could serve any church, which we all know is not true anymore because we are already a very diverse denomination regarding our church practices. Working within the cabinet for even one week, you learn to appreciate the diversity of the body of Christ. God must love diversity, because God sure does make a lot of different kinds of people and ultimately, churches.

A new form of unity could provide an opportunity for the church to be better positioned for the 21st century. It's been said that you should never let a serious crisis go to waste. The crisis has hit, and in time, we may discover opportunities to restructure ourselves in a way that might allow multiple branches of the church to flourish and reach even more people for Jesus Christ for the transformation of the world through the Wesleyan Way. The lingering question for 2020 may be, *Where does the emerging leadership come from, which people will tbe trusted enough to envision a new form of governance and a new understanding of what Methodism looks like globally?* We all will have to come to grips that unity is not uniformity. I would contend that we have never had uniformity in The United Methodist Church except around the articles of religion and our structure, which is interpreted and practiced differently around the world. I still believe the Wesleyan Way is the best way to promote Christianity and I will work with a hopeful and generous spirit to make that so.

**Robert Farr** serves as Bishop of the Missouri Area of The United Methodist Church. He has authored or co-authored several books including: *Renovate or Die - 10 Ways to Focus Your Church in Mission* (2011), *Get Their Name- Grow Your Church by Building New Relationships* (2013), *10 Prescriptions for a Healthy Church* (2015), *The Necessary Nine* (2015) and *Obvious Wisdom* (2018). He is a certified Fire Chaplain through Global Board of Higher Education and Ministry.

Photo by Kevin Slimp, Market Square Books

On Sundays following the 2019 General Conference, congregations throughout United Methodism gathered for worship.

# CHAPTER ELEVEN

# Thomas Edward Frank
To Redefine our Present Connectionality:
Thoughts on a Way Beyond the Way Forward

When I was ordained a Deacon forty-seven years ago, I never dreamed that my entire life as an ordained minister, teacher, and scholar would be shadowed by the divisive tactics of a sectarian group within the denomination. As the years have gone by, I have increasingly tried to intervene in the situation any way I could – through the classroom, as consultant to the Council of Bishops, and as a member or consultant of three different Ministry Study Commissions authorized by General Conference, but to no avail. I've also come to realize over time that the generations coming along behind me do not particularly want the denominational structure, polity, or culture that they are inheriting. That's how it should be: every generation must make their stamp on how we work together as Methodist people. What follows are my reflections and suggestions for those whose task and privilege it will be to create whatever comes next.

## A Little History
*Sex and Power*

Early on the morning of November 19, 2014, I was rushing to the airport to fly to Philadelphia. I had been talking with the Rev. Frank Schaefer's defense team by conference call regularly over the past few months, but now it was time to actually go testify as an expert witness to interpret the *Book of Discipline* at his church trial.

Everything about this trial was wrong from the beginning. A charge should never have been brought against Frank Schaefer for performing the wedding of his own son to the man he loved. Only a month remained until the statute of limitations expired. The complaint had been brought by a non-resident member of Frank's congregation who was angry over changes that had been made in the church. The situation cried out for a just resolution process. But the bishops had been getting some seriously misguided legal advice from civil attorneys, essentially denying them the full range of their episcopal powers and telling them that they had to bring charges that lead to trials. And so, a trial was underway.

My host picked me up at the airport and we drove about fifty miles into the countryside west of Philadelphia, to the much-beloved UM Camp Innabah. This had also been the site of the church trial that threw Beth Stroud out of the ministry, at the very church camp where she had grown up as a young United Methodist. Turning off a country road, we came over the crest of a hill and pulled into a parking lot. Several men and women in bright yellow vests carrying walkie-talkies were guarding the lot and buildings, asking for credentials and guiding people where they needed to go. From what I could gather, they were all lay people from local churches who volunteered for this ugly but necessary duty.

I was called to testify and was escorted up the hill to the camp gymnasium. I walked in through the roped-off spectator area, down a center aisle, past the rows of chairs all packed with observers and reporters sitting quietly. I was directed to sit in a slightly raised chair, which was ahead of me and slightly to my right. To get there I had to pass a table on my right for the counsel for the church and the complainant, a table on my left for Frank's defense team, a double row of chairs on my right angled toward the front and roped off, where the thirteen clergy comprising the trial court sat, and then directly ahead of me the presiding bishop and his advising counsel on a raised platform at the center. After I sat down, I noticed a court reporter typing the proceedings into one of those machines they use in courtrooms.

And it struck me – and struck me hard – that this was not going to be a conversation. There would be no exchange of facts and interpretations and ideas. Gone was the ingrained UM practice of sitting in Christian conversation around a table, truly trying to understand each other's views, getting to know each other's backgrounds, and trying to find a way to continue our ministries together. Conversation was over. This was a trial. In this completely open room that had no fixed furniture – a room that could have been set up any way the church wanted to set it up – the church set it up as an exact replica of *Law and Order*. In fact, the parlance of everyone I chatted with at the trial, the reporters who called me, everybody just talked readily about the prosecution, the defense, the judge, and the jury, witnesses, evidence, testimony, sentence – mostly terms which do not appear in the *Discipline* but which deeply shape the church's imagination for what it's doing in these circumstances.

At this point the trial court had already found Frank "guilty" not only of performing a same-sex marriage, but of "disobedience to the order and discipline of the church." I was there to testify about the meaning of these charges and thus to provide some context for the trial court to think about what would be an appropriate sanction for Frank. Oddly, and I think inexcusably, the presiding bishop (again getting bad legal advice based in civil, not church, law) did not permit me to testify at an earlier stage about what the charges meant and thus to make any contribution to the trial court's thinking about whether to find Frank guilty. When I stepped down after "testifying," I sat in the audience for a few minutes. I really wanted to hear Tim Schaefer, who was up next. He told the story of his life, his fears of ruining his father's career, his teenage thoughts of suicide, his thrill at the hugs and love and acceptance of his family when he came out to them, and then at finding a man he loved, his gratitude and love for his father who came to perform his ceremony. You would have to have a heart of stone not to be moved, even to have your life and attitudes completely transformed, by what Tim said that day.

> *"Stepping down that hill toward the parking lot, I was overwhelmed with grief for what had become of the church into which I was ordained."*

But the *Discipline* has been turned into a book of stone, and of course, nothing made any difference in the end. I had to catch my return flight. With tears welling up in my eyes, I walked back through that audience and out into the sunny, cold, and windy afternoon. Stepping down that hill toward the parking lot, I was overwhelmed with grief for what had become of the church into which I was ordained.

I was ordained deacon in the Missouri East Conference in 1972. My ordination was only about a month after the conclusion of General Conference in Atlanta, where I had started seminary at Candler. An excited seminarian, I had attended several sessions of the conference. I was there the day the final draft of the Social Principles was brought to the floor for adoption. Reflecting compassion for the way homosexuals were discriminated against in church and society, the Principles draft named homosexuals as "persons of sacred worth" and insisted on their "human and civil rights." The draft did not venture into norms and values about homosexuality, only addressing the plight of homosexual persons in the society of the time.

This was not enough for some delegates. In a well-orchestrated strategy of parliamentary maneuvers and amendments, they took it upon themselves to introduce a moral judgment into the paragraph – that the "practice" of homosexuality was "incompatible with Christian teaching." Actually, at first the amendment said "doctrine" but the amenders accepted a change to "teaching."

Was this dropping of a "doctrine" claim a tacit recognition that the UMC actually had done utterly and absolutely no study of human sexuality and had no current understanding of any church teaching about it? As the wise scholar Walter Muelder from Boston University said on the floor that day, "homosexuality is a very emotional question . . . our church as a whole has not yet matured in its thought on this very complex matter." But some people apparently assumed they did have mature thoughts, and playing on the unexamined prejudices of the delegates, got the amendment passed.

Muelder had urged the delegates not to "prejudge a future thinking in our church on its social principles," and was that warning ever prophetic! Once this ill-considered statement was adopted, the UMC entered into a living hell of now forty-seven years of conflict, little of which has ever been informed by serious study or, more to the point, by earnest conversation among those who disagree.

Twelve years later, the original prejudgment was compounded in Baltimore 1984. Here again, a General Conference commission on ministry put forward only the now-familiar language that even they referred to as the so-called "seven last words:" fidelity in marriage and celibacy in singleness. But this, too, was not enough. Led by political strategists, a minority report was presented denying ordination to "self-avowed practicing homosexuals," and perhaps even more tellingly, locating the sentence in the paragraph about ordained persons being "subject to all the frailties of the human condition and pressures of society" but being held to "the highest standards of holy living in the world." Thus, again without any study or serious conversation, under the influence of a well-organized campaign, delegates voted 525-442 to associate homosexuality with moral failings. And unbelievably thirty-five years later, that paragraph remains.

All of these flagship phrases contain a raft of inner contradictions that the Judicial Council, bishops, district superintendents, and the rank and file have spent decades trying to sort out. What, for example, is a "practicing" homosexual? Does it mean having affection for a person of your same gender? Does it include holding hands? Sharing a house? What, for that matter, is a "practicing" heterosexual? Aren't we just all full human beings?

The sorry tale of unexamined prejudices reached its peak – and I'd like to think its tipping point – exactly 15 years ago in Ft. Worth 2004. This General Conference, by an agonizing margin of only ten votes, declared both the practice of homosexuality and the performance of a homosexual union or a same-sex wedding to be stand-alone chargeable offenses. I'm not sure how much everybody understands what an unprecedented step this was. A well-organized campaign persuaded a bare majority of delegates to remove all room for serious conversation or pastoral judgment. Little wonder that we have now embarked on an era of trials previously unknown in our tradition.

> *"I have wondered why so many UM's have been silent while this virulent campaign of control over our denomination has marched on."*

I've been puzzled by a number of things over all these years of divisive and ill-considered legislation. I have wondered why most pastors, whatever their understanding about homosexuality, have stood by while General Conference strayed into the territory of limiting pastoral judgment and pastoral action.

I have wondered why so many UM's have been silent while this virulent campaign of control over our denomination has marched on. We have witnessed, for example, organized campaigns for slates of General Conference delegates, including many with no experience and no real interest in the *Discipline* except for two or three sentences; substitution of thoroughly vetted nominations for Judicial Council with little known persons nominated from the floor; and a virtually unprecedented vote of the Council of Bishops to request a formal complaint against one of their own.

While our polity was being twisted and warped with unconstitutional insertions, poor language and double-speak (you can have sacred worth but not "practice"), I have wondered how many people are noticing that the vast majority of the campaigners and supporters of this campaign are older "white" men. What's up with that? What's going on with the "white" men? (I put quotes around "white" now in everything I write, because it continues to be among the most unexamined and presumptive terms in the vocabulary of "white" power and superiority.)

Is it just a coincidence that 1972 was also the year when the merger of "white" annual conferences with the annual conferences created by the black Central Jurisdiction under the Methodist apartheid system was almost, agonizingly complete? Is it a coincidence

that 1972 was the same year the General Conference voted to create
a Commission on Religion and Race to advocate for justice and full
participation in the newly multiracial church? Or that General
Conference also voted to create a Commission on the Status and
Role of Women? Or that the specific prohibitions against divorce,
remarriage after divorce, ordination of divorced persons, and
investigation of any clergy who got a divorce, were finally replaced
by the Social Principles' statements on the painful necessity of
divorce under some circumstances?

The world of "white male privilege" was being shaken to its
roots, stirring anger and hostility and fear for identity – deep
antagonisms to which Fox "News" and like-minded mouthpieces
are continuing testimony. Who remained now who could finally be
excluded? The church, led by "white" men, picked the least powerful, often most despised, and yet in many cases the most devout,
loyal, and active longtime members of congregations, to be the
scapegoat for a world of change in which the old order could never
be recovered.

It becomes clearer with every passing year how much the
crusade to isolate and limit homosexuality (without ever actually
defining it) in the church was a crusade for power. One of its basic
tools was the rhetoric of crisis that has continued relentlessly right
up to the present day. From the very first decade of the crusade
against homosexuality, the basic argument in support of the new
legalism on sex was the fear of losing people. In 1972 the UMC
was only five years in to what would become a consistent trend
of having fewer total members each year than the year before.
Clearly there were major shifts in American culture affecting
every religious group.

But advocates of the new church laws were not interested in
wider trends. They needed to insist that the UMC was "losing"
members, that people were "leaving" because of changes in the
church (even though this factor has never been statistically significant), and that accepting homosexuality would be the last straw:
we would "lose" even more. These threats of decline and loss – the
drumbeat of the rhetoric of crisis – became a lever of power that
has twisted and diminished our Wesleyan heritage as a church
that truly welcomes all who come seeking God.

I wrote a letter to a bishop (a "white" guy) back in the 1990s,
reminding him that we'd known each other for many years, and
just asking him how he could in good conscience support the
church's so-called "stand" on homosexuality. I said, "Look, I'm
a born-and-bred Methodist and I've known gay and lesbian lay
people in every church I've served. I know many gay and lesbian

pastors. We are already all part of the connection, all in the Methodist family, so how can you deny our fellow Christians their place in the church? He wrote back a detailed letter for which I give him credit – he took the time – but the only thing I remember about it was the long paragraph about anal sex. He was against it. When I could finally catch my breath – no bishop had ever addressed me on the subject of anal sex before – I got to thinking. Who said anything about anal sex? What is this really all about? From the time of the scriptures until now, what is said against homosexuality is said by men, and about men. Even a *lesbian* woman can't get equal time. So, is the church to be governed and distorted by men and their fears and secrets?

One of the worst consequences of the campaign against full participation of the full range of human sexuality is its ideological distortion of our tradition. Co-opting the Wesley or Aldersgate name for their cause, the boundary keepers have steadily dragged the denomination into exactly the sectarianism that Wesley would have abhorred.

John Wesley was a child of the Church of England, into which he was ordained, and to which he was loyal to his dying day. He was formed in a national church that was created to embrace as many viewpoints as possible in an often-fractured land. His church was a middle way, a *via media*, between estrangements and polarizations. Methodism, necessarily independent in a new land without a national church, inherited that mantle of the middle way in the American colonies.

This *via media* character explains why we have so infrequently tried to put boundaries around pastoral action and judgment, and certainly explains why we have never been any good at kicking people out. The legalism and litigious atmosphere of our polity in recent years is so unlike us. As I keep telling reporters who ask, we just don't do trials. We want everyone to stay.

The *via media* is why I have never been able to understand why the church's struggle with homosexuality should be a church-dividing issue. To stay together around contentious questions requires earnest conversation. Good News, the Confessing Movement, UMACTION, and the insidious outside Political Action Committee labeled the "Institute for Religion and Democracy" (which I prefer to call the "Bureau of Ideology and Absolutism") regularly claim that the anti-gay legislation is the product of "Christian conversation." If that ever occurred as part of their well-funded political campaigns, I missed it. They should "man up" and take responsibility for the fact that they have succeeded.

They have effectively organized blatant political campaigns previously unknown to this church of the middle. They have won! They got this stuff put in the book and they've gone all-out to get this stuff enforced. And, they have been astonishingly successful at shutting down the conversation. As I've traveled the connection over these years, I have heard little open conversation about this subject. In most annual conferences, it has not appeared safe to question the church's laws publicly. We have been cursed with a cloak of silence that has exacerbated the pervasive passive-aggressive culture of our denomination.

Only now, in 2019, aghast at the continued absolutism of the "victors," has a broad swath of people spoken out loudly and clearly. Even folks who are not sure what they think about human sexuality are put off by the cheesy tactics of the radical sectarians: handing out free cell phones, or this year, free iPads, to delegates from outside the US, pre-loaded with pointers on how to vote. (And if you want to discuss it, come to our free breakfast where we will tell you what to do.)

I think we have crossed a threshold of tolerance for this un-Wesleyan absolutism, from which there is no turning back now. It is time for something new.

## A Little Polity

*Could we please write a new Discipline?*

The *Book of Discipline* of the UMC in its current form has had a good run. It is a product of the twentieth century development of the denomination as an American non-profit voluntary association, a national organization of considerable reach into nearly every county of the United States. As one of the two largest Protestant denominations in the US, United Methodism has had an expansive self-image of potency and influence in American society. The *Discipline* has expanded in parallel, elaborating the relative powers and duties of laity and clergy who hold office in the church, and adding more and more measures of structure, responsibilities, and accountability of the agencies created by General Conference for shared ministry and mission (the latter occupying well over 200 pages in the current book).

Over the last thirty years, this expansiveness has extended around the world, as annual conferences of Methodists in Russia, Eastern Europe, parts of Africa, and the Philippines have been voted into membership of the denomination. That is, they have moved from being mission partners in the Wesleyan tradition to being voting delegates and members in the governing bodies of the denomination under the *Discipline* as published in the US.

Over that same thirty years, the UMC as an organization has continued to be obsessed with being big, and with retaining its national and global clout. The Call to Action report that came forward in 2012 took this rhetoric to a new level, claiming a vision that the UMC would be the "world leader" in "making disciples of Jesus Christ." I take that moment to be the ultimate illusion of hubris and self-importance from which the church now has the opportunity to wake up.

> *"Only now, in 2019, aghast at the continued absolutism of the "victors," has a broad swath of people spoken out loudly and clearly."*

The *Discipline* in its current form has had its day. It is time for a much shorter book that focuses on the most basic elements of shared governance and oversight. We need a *Discipline* that puts the *principle of subsidiarity* in the forefront, moving most authority to the people and places where an action has the most immediate impact.

The era now ending has produced a great deal of poorly conceived and poorly written legislation, and several of the most unhinged Judicial Council decisions in memory. We could begin with the fact that the legislation against the full humanity of all persons regardless of sexuality hangs on a phrase in the Social Principles, which are explicitly not church law and never have been. The legislation that has been adopted is in blatant contradiction to Article 4 of the Constitution. No organization can put in their constitution a statement that all persons are "eligible" for membership and full participation, and then turn around and insert into legislative paragraphs statements excluding a certain ill-defined class of persons. Yet, no Judicial Council has ever had occasion to state this obvious point.

Already slogging through the mire of excessive legislative paragraphs telling everybody what to do (or what they can't do), the church and its officers have spent ungodly amounts of time parsing the words "self-avowed practicing homosexual" not to mention the odd word "celibacy" (when did Methodist ministry become a monastic order?). To help everyone cut to the chase, the Judicial Council, in an opinion written by the Rev. Keith Boyette, now president of the sectarian Wesleyan Covenant Association, took it upon itself to supply definitions that can only be called pornographic and voyeuristic – a weirdly twisted tease of male sexual fantasies. But in any case, the Judicial Council cannot write legislation, making that opinion, too, invalid.

Sex isn't the only subject over which the *Discipline* is tied in knots. The Connectional Table, described in some of the most indecipherable generalities in the book, has no constitutional authority for the responsibilities assigned to it. This has created immense confusion about its institutional role. Similarly, the phrase "making disciples of Jesus Christ for the transformation of the world" has been stuck into every section of the book, even as the meaning of the phrase and its translation into expectations of various offices and agencies of the church goes unexplained.

The book never interprets what is meant by a "disciple," or what it would mean to "make" one. But here is that hubris again, the presumption that the church can "make" a disciple and know what it's doing when it "makes" one (It's important to note the word "make" cannot be justified as a translation of the Greek in that verse. It's a clumsy Anglicizing of the original).

In short, the *Discipline* has grown into a jumble of competing expectations, aspirations, and intentions, jarringly combined with legalisms that suck the church into a quagmire of conflict. It is time for a do-over. This means it's time for a new denominational entity to carry Methodism into the coming decades.

## Disentangling the New Discipline From the Past

Here are five ways in which a new *Discipline* must disentangle the church from both *Disciplinary* and civil laws of the past:

### 1. Terminate the futile attempt to create a global denomination with common governance.

Continuing and deepening global bonds of shared community and mission, grounded in the Wesleyan tradition, should be the primary force that draws us into one family of churches. Shared governance is impossible.

The long-established institutions of the denomination, from general agencies to theological schools to local churches, originated in the US under conditions of an emerging American culture and the American experiment of representative democracy. Delegates from other nations, who have voting powers over these institutions but little knowledge of their origins or practices, cannot make informed decisions. Many come from nations with little or no heritage of democracy as it is understood in the West. Many have never been part of any kind of governance group in which they could actually have a voice. This leaves them vulnerable to the political machinations of groups that make promises and trade-offs in exchange for guiding their votes.

The perfectly understandable lack of comprehension of petitions brought forward by Americans has been a source of light-hearted humor for a long time. I still remember a Swedish pastor asking me to explain what "servant leadership" meant, but it's not funny anymore. Not after the nightmare of voting in St. Louis on a matter that should have no standing as church law applying to all nations. Add to this the wide variations in the understanding of property held by the church under various legal systems, and diverse roles of the church in various societies, and it quickly becomes obvious that trying to have a common discipline is neither practical or useful. Further, the UMC soon will simply no longer have resources to fund the expenses of global General Conferences and global representation in every arm of General Conference.

Many Methodist churches around the world are not part of the UMC. Why shouldn't churches of every nation have autonomy in governance while sharing in the common ministries of Methodism around the world?

### 2. Terminate the denominational relationship with at least 15,000 local churches in the United States.

The denomination is stretched enough in human and financial resources without taking responsibility for the thousands of chapels, meeting houses, and small-membership congregations that dot the landscape. Many are a remnant of the settlement patterns of 19th-century America. Many are sustained by one or two donors or families, and few have any prospect of growing in ministry. Does this mean that they should be closed? By no means. But they should be set loose to sustain their own continuation and find their own worship leadership. They should take over their own buildings (many have been some other tradition before they were Methodist in any case) and fulfill the ministry they see for themselves. These churches generally have fewer than fifty people in worship, certainly not sufficient to merit pastoral appointments or the inordinate amount of time spent trying to supply them with preachers. They constitute an enormous burden that a new denomination simply cannot be carrying into the future.

Because the Discipline grants no one in particular the authority to close or separate from local churches, the UMC continues to prop them open. It has allowed itself to drift into becoming a denomination of local pastors and a myriad of other categories of preacher, whose authority few people can interpret. In some annual conferences, local pastors far outnumber the ordained ministers. We now have somewhere around 8000+ local pastors across the US. No one in any way is questioning their calling. But it is certainly legitimate to ask if they are well enough trained to carry on ministry in the Wesleyan tradition. I have taught in local pastor's schools and led events with many local pastors participating. All too many express a theology that is Calvinist or Reformed, not Wesleyan. Many, despite our best efforts to determine qualifications, are fundamentalists in theology and teaching. That's fine if that's their vocation, but why does the UMC invest so much in them?

I estimate that there are about 11,000 local church congregations in the US that are viable, and that can marshal the human and financial resources to function as a constituted local church with an identifiable ministry and mission in the place they serve. This is still a very large number compared to other Protestant denominations. Again, a future Methodism must get over its obsession with BIG, with being omnipresent in society and pretending to have the resources to oversee this religious empire. This model is plainly not sustainable. Set people free with their buildings and their local pastors to pursue their own work. They do not need to be part of a new denominational organization.

3. **Terminate the general agencies authorized by General Conference in their present form and enable those with substantive programming to continue as non-profit organizations.**

102

Put the powers and duties of the General Board of Higher Education and Ministry alongside the number of valiant staff trying to carry them out, and one quickly realizes the impossibility, even absurdity, of these expectations. Look at the programs of the General Board of Discipleship and ask yourself what could not be done just as well if it were a non-profit consulting agency for local church ministries. Allow annual conferences to organize their own initiatives and turn to these non-profits for resources. Use existing endowed funds accrued by general agencies over generations to support the new non-profits and their initiatives for budding ministries anywhere in the world. By this action alone, over 200 pages of the *Discipline* will go away.

**4. Terminate the legal ties of the denomination with universities, colleges, schools, and seminaries.**

The UMC simply does not have the human or financial resources to play a meaningful role in institutions, many of which were founded a century or more ago and have developed their own distinct ways of carrying out education grounded in the Wesleyan tradition. Emerging global universities such as SMU, Emory, Duke, Northwestern, and Boston have expanded their programs and reach vastly beyond their founding years, when their presidents were uniformly male Methodist clergy, and their boards of trustees entirely, or mainly, Methodist. Schools of theology have become widely ecumenical in faculty and student body. Far from threatening the Wesleyan heritage, this diversity strengthens the unique perspectives and gifts of our heritage. In virtually every UM-affiliated educational institution, the 2019 General Conference vote flew directly in the face of their culture and ethos, their values and aspirations. The denomination continues to delude itself that it has the power and influence to send visiting committees as a kind of continuing accreditation of Wesleyan credentials in these

schools (that hubris again). Many of these campus visitors simply have no idea what to ask or how to grasp the scale of these schools. And why should they? Let the institutions loose from legal and official affiliation (and in some cases, charters under state law and jurisdiction). After all, didn't the church found institutions like hospitals, homes, schools, and colleges in order to set them free to have a transformative effect on the public welfare of the society? Let them go do their work!

Then, take the money freed up from obligations created by church law and create a foundation(s) to which institutions can apply for grants to support initiatives that advance their mission. Having taught in both a UM school of theology and an ecumenical unaffiliated school, I can say without question that the openness of spirit, and the freedom to choose in what forms to relate school and denomination with each other, is healthier for both sides in an unaffiliated school.

5. **Write a minimalist *Book of Discipline* that contains only the key sentences of definition or authorization. Avoid the temptation to write a *Discipline* that tells everyone what to do.**

Part of the downfall of the UMC Discipline has been its length. It is overwritten, with too many sentences that could be interpreted as mandates. The chapter on ordained ministry offers a prime example. The authority to decide who is called and qualified for ordination constitutionally lies with the annual conference. This is where it properly belongs, close to the local churches and ministries that will be served, close to the candidates who in many cases have been residents in that region for much of their lives. The sentences added in 1984 to prevent boards of ordained ministry and annual conferences from considering candidates who "practice" "homosexuality" sent a distinct chill into this constitutional principle. Instead of being free to consider candidates on their own merits, boards wasted untold hours trying to meet a requirement that is deeply offensive to the full humanity of people regardless of their sexuality.

Still, this was only the most egregious example of overreach by General Conference. What in some ways opened the door for the homosexuality sentences was the proliferation of mandates for boards and candidates: pages with lists of questions to be asked, lists of courses that must be taken, and a rigid process for even being considered as a candidate that has driven away many prospective ordinands. General Conference even decided to tell theological schools what to teach, without having any conversatios with the schools or their faculties. The last straw was the addition of a mandated course in "evangelism," which again remains undefined, forcing schools to create a nonexistent academic field indistinguishable from the already-tenuous "field" of missiology.

There is absolutely no reason for General Conference to extend its legislative powers into these areas. It communicates a lack of trust. It induces passive-aggressive reactions. It suggests that members of our common covenant cannot be allowed the freedom to create their own culture and practice of education and ministry appropriate to the people of their region.

But this is only one example of unnecessary verbiage. The Discipline is rife with a mish-mash of paragraphs from study commission reports, sections and chapters beginning with unnumbered paragraphs which make it impossible to determine if they are part of church law or not, and sentences that are aspirational rather than legislative. Cut, cut, cut – and we can have a much leaner *Discipline* and more responsibilities closer to the local church.

Are these proposals a downsizing of the denomination? Yes. Do they represent a diminishment in ministry and mission? No. They simply move authority for ministry closer to where it is practiced. Do they suggest abandoning the global church? Hardly. The stronger the local church everywhere, the stronger the global becomes. We do not need a global denomination. But we do need a lean, healthy, and resourceful US denomination that can advance the ministries of its own churches and share in mission with churches around the world.

These are some of the challenges that the next generations must face and rise to the occasion of writing a common covenant. Few people have shown any inclination to master the constitutional principles and legislative content of the current book. I hope that the opportunity to craft something new for the future will offer a space for new talents, new wisdom, and new approaches for the church that is to come.

**Thomas Edward Frank** is University Professor and Chair of the Department of History at Wake Forest University in Winston-Salem, North Carolina.

Dr. Frank's publications include a study of the relationship of Protestant Christianity and the liberal arts college in his *Theology, Ethics, and the Nineteenth Century American College Ideal* (Mellen 1993). He has written extensively on the culture and place of American congregations; his book *The Soul of the Congregation* (Abingdon 2000) exploring congregational narrative and sense of place is widely used in clergy education. Author of the standard textbook on the evolution and practice of United Methodist polity and organization, *Polity, Practice, and the Mission of The United Methodist Church* (3rd Ed., Abingdon 2006), he has written polity articles for the *Encyclopedia of Religion in America* (2010), the *Oxford Handbook of Methodist Studies* (2009) and the *T and T Clark Companion to Methodism* (2010), and co-authored with Russell E. Richey *Episcopacy in Methodist Tradition: Perspectives and Proposals* (Abingdon 2004).

# CHAPTER TWELVE
# Erin M. Hawkins
An Inevitable Awakening of the Human Family

> The Spirit of the Sovereign LORD is upon me, for
> the LORD has anointed me to bring good news to the poor.
> He has sent me to comfort the brokenhearted and to proclaim
> that captives will be released and prisoners will be freed.
>
> **Isaiah 61:1 (NLT)**

In April 1968, a newly formed United Methodist Church changed its practice of sanctioned discrimination and institutionalized segregation by ending the Central Jurisdiction which separated blacks and whites in the Methodist Episcopal Church. This action was taken in part, due to the insistence of the Evangelical United Brethren Church, which proclaimed that it would not merge with Methodists if we held firm in our practice of systemic racism.

Fifty years later, the action of the Special Called Session of General Conference to support the Traditional Plan serves as proof that our comfort with sanctioned discrimination and exclusion has never left. The sin of white supremacy which has plagued the Methodist movement from its inception continues to reveal its dominance within both conservative and progressive camps of the Church.

My heart grieves for my Lesbian, Gay, Bisexual, Transgender, Queer, Intersex, and Asexual (LGBTQIA+) siblings who experienced the harm of continued rejection, insensitive and bigoted rhetoric, and emotional and spiritual disregard. I acknowledge your dedication to the church in spite of the oppression you face and respect any feelings of anger or betrayal that may lead some of you to walk away.

I also grieve for those Traditionalists whose willingness to be in authentic dialogue and relationship was overshadowed by forces that corrupted the work of the General Conference.

## Here's What I Know as a Woman of Color

Despite the changes of law in 1968, which intended to end the exclusion of blacks and other people of color in the life and witness of the church, systemic racism still plagues us. There are churches in the connection that still resist the appointment of pastors of color and actively reject their leadership. There are still Boards of Ordained Ministry and Cabinets who execute racial double standards in the credentialing of candidates for ordination and appointment. There is still a lack of focused attention in the denomination to reach growing communities of color in the United States, and by extension, to speak consistently and relevantly to the racial injustices that confront our world. Women are still seeking a change in The United Methodist Constitution to "guarantee" their inclusion. Simply put, changes in United Methodist law, while an essential first step, have not resulted in full inclusion for people of color and will not result in full inclusion for LGBTQIA+ people, either.

There were Pharisees in Matthew 22 who sought to build a trap for Jesus using the law. To them, he replied that loving God and loving neighbor were the two greatest commandments on which all other laws and prophets hinged. Using the law as a weapon is an age-old tactic and Jesus reminds us even now that Love IS the law!

## Our True Mission

The struggle to end oppression in all of its forms and to realize the vision of full inclusion must continue. AND... at the end of the day, changing the law is simply a means to an end. Our true mission is to make love real in a church and world that needs it now more than ever. The love that I am talking about :

- A love that actively honors freedom and won't allow the *Book of Discipline* to hold us back from calling justice to roll down like a river and righteousness like an ever-flowing stream.

- A love that actively honors humility and calls us to repent for how we decry some forms of oppression while remaining silent about or participating in others.

- A love that actively honors community and binds us together as the true church, the fellowship of all believers, where we hold one another accountable and no one is alienated, excluded, or left behind.

- A love that actively honors humanity and challenges us to realize that our focus on what happens in the church is not an excuse to ignore what is happening outside of the church. If we cannot be a church present in the world, then we are not the church.

- A love that actively honors self and invites each of us to "do our work." It is time for all people who experience oppression and those who support them, to confront our own biases (implicit and explicit) and get the support we need to heal our traumas, unhealthy need for external validation and addictions to mental, physical, and emotional pain that prevent us from living our best God-ordained lives right now. Our greatest hope for liberation lies in our own unfettered joy, courageous vulnerability, purposeful self-expression, and sacred action.

And most importantly, a love of God who calls us to move past our superficial interpretations of love to a depth of generosity, unconditional acceptance, and passionate pursuit of wholeness that can only come from abiding in the eternal truth of love that is God.

I am committed to doing all that I can as a leader in this church to continue challenging the laws that oppress. In my heart, however, I know that I am called to more. I must make the aim of my living and leadership to make real, in every way possible, a liberating love that transforms the world and every human being in it.

The contraction, resistance, and breaking open that is taking place in the denomination right now is so much bigger than The United Methodist Church. What we are experiencing is, in a small way, the messy but inevitable awakening of the human family.

### *Let the birthing continue...*

**Ms. Erin M. Hawkins** is General Secretary of the General Commission on Religion and Race. She is lead official of the denominational agency that cultivates racial inclusion and the full participation of all people into the work, witness, and life of The UMC. GCORR empowers church clergy and lay leadership to utilize the values of inclusion, racial equity, and justice in the transformative work of vital congregations in order to build up the body of Christ.

Ms. Hawkins works to share lessons in creating holy relationship with God by, "holding in tension our capacity for greatness that calls us, as Christians, to persevere in the struggle towards becoming our better selves, and to combat our worst tendencies of racism, sexism, and classism."

# CHAPTER THIRTEEN
# Donald Haynes

Is the United Methodist "Ice Cube" Melting?

My mother–in-law had a saying which she repeated when situations were complex, confusing, unprecedented, or fearsome. She would say, "Worst mess I ever saw."

Her maxim came to mind when I downloaded and read the minutes and various commentaries on United Methodism's acrimonious General Conference in St. Louis! My career is long. I was first appointed as a student pastor in 1954, the year of the United States Supreme Court decision, "Brown vs. Topeka Board of Education." I remember so well going to a district meeting at which our District Superintendent said to our southern audience, "Integration is now the law of the land. This decision affects not only our public schools, but must affect our churches. We are law abiding citizens." I went back to my rural parish, told them what he said, and quoted Jesus and our invitational policy: "Whosoever will may come."

Whatever personal conviction one might have about the decisions made by the UMC General Conference, the fact is that the Traditional Plan passed and it is the "law of the church." Subsequently, the Judicial Council has ruled that eight of the fourteen amendments to the Book of Discipline are constitutional. This is where we are, and we arrived by a closely scrutinized process. The bishops who presided did a superb job under stress.

Since the late nineteenth century, Methodists have allowed, and often embraced, a measure of doctrinal pluralism under the umbrella of John Wesley's famous dictum, "If your heart is as mine, give me your hand." However, with regard to polity, the "Books of Discipline" of the several Wesleyan bodies have been interpreted as mandatory. Except for some latitude with the Social Principles and Book of Resolutions, we have constantly cited the Book of Discipline as ecclesiastical law that must be obeyed.

The UMC denominational leadership promoted the One Church Plan very effectively. Tom Berlin from Virginia made a video explaining the One Church Plan that was recommended by the Way Forward Commission and the overwhelming majority of the bishops. On the floor of General Conference, the voices of opposition to the Traditional Plan were more strident than silent.

On the floor, Berlin spoke somewhat apocalyptically:

> "What is being said in private conversation is that if the 'TP' is voted in today, you will be putting a virus into the American Church that will make it very sick, and make it sick quickly. Many of us have members who will leave. Many pastors are going to lead their churches away from the connection. Some conferences will leave; others will stay and fight, and they will do weddings. They will break the Book of Discipline... The organizational model, the economic model will all be sick. If you cannot support the One Church Plan, simply abstain. Wash your hands of this Traditional Plan today because it will be an illness to our house."

Adam Hamilton, whose many books have been used as study books in the great majority of UMC churches, spoke against the Traditional Plan. He castigated the Wesleyan Christian Association (WCA):

> "The last five years you have asked for, and been planning for, an amicable separation. I thought you wanted to leave; now it appears you want the rest of us to leave. Centrist and progressives never wanted a divorce; we never looked for a gracious exit. You've inspired an awful lot of people who (were) not engaged in the struggle before, and for that I thank you. You've invited them to action. They're mad. They're upset. They're hurt."

After some biblical exegesis, Hamilton concluded,

> "There are three texts in the New Testament that speak of some kind of same-sex acts. There are over a hundred that call for unity and working to stay together. I want to finally ask this: If you voted for the Simple Plan or the One Church Plan, would you please stand, and bishops, I'd like to ask if you'd do the same."

Uncounted estimates are that two-thirds of the U.S. delegates stood. One youth delegate referred to her and her friends' having received over 15,000 messages from back home pleading for the defeat of the Traditional Plan.

Kim Ingram, Director of Ministerial Services and Conference

Secretary in Western North Carolina, coaches scores of seminary students in their journey toward ordination. Kim is a member of the University Senate. She spoke in behalf of the seminarians from whom she had heard:

> "It is clear to the heads of our seminaries that if the Traditional Plan passes, many students will decide there is no place for them in this denomination. If the TP passes, we will very soon lose an entire generation of leadership in the United States. This may not be true in Africa or elsewhere, but the future of the UMC in this country is at stake."

*"Meanwhile, Jesus weeps over the catfight among Wesley's progeny. "O Lord of hosts, be with us yet."*

Voices of support for the Traditional Plan were also heard. They reflected the reality of The United Methodist Church's being a global church. In Africa, where United Methodism is growing rapidly, the support of the Traditional Plan is overwhelming. Dr. Jerry Kulah, Dean of the Gbarnga School of Theology at The United Methodist University in Liberia, asked that the African delegates not be treated as children. He affirmed strongly that the African United Methodists know their conscience and will vote it:

> "I want to establish that The United Methodist Church is not a United States Church. We are struggling against Islamic forces and other religious bodies in Africa and other parts of the world. So, we cannot attempt to do anything but support the Traditional Plan because it is indeed the biblical plan."

At a Good News Briefing Breakfast, Dr. Kulah pushed back against the accusation that African votes were being bought. "If anyone is so naïve or condescending to think we Africans would sell our birthright in Jesus Christ for American dollars, then they simply do not know us."

Delegates from Eurasian nations that were once in the Soviet Union and delegates from the Philippines spoke similarly. Cultures in Africa, Eurasia, and southeast Asia are influenced by Islamic prohibition of homosexual lifestyles or orientation.

Aislinn Devioney from the Rio Texas Conference spoke for the TP:

> "We all have friends and family in the LGBTQIA+ community that we love and we value as brothers and sisters. Contrary to

the messages ... at this conference, we have found ways to get along and to live in relationship with each other. Our desire is to serve in ministry alongside each other, a representation of the reconciling work of God. We are passionate about our Wesleyan heritage, uniting head and heart, cultivating personal and social holiness, and carefully balancing grace and truth. It may be easy for onlookers to believe that the church is void of voices like ours. That is not true. There are thousands of us in your local churches fiercely committed to a traditional definition of marriage."

After much parliamentary posturing, the presiding bishop called for the official vote on the Traditional Plan. Following procedural votes in setting the agenda and voting as a legislative committee, the plenary session passed by 53-47 percent the Traditional Plan, which was designed and edited by a populist group. The governing body of The United Methodist Church had spoken.

After the secret ballot votes appeared on the screens, David Livingston from the Great Plains Conference made these remarks:

"Traditionalists made the original exit plan. Traditionalists passed their plan. This is their exit. This is not my exit. This is not an exit for Progressives. And Traditionalists, if you wanna take your exit, you can take your exit, and I'm gonna give it to you, but we will not leave this church of Jesus Christ."

Livingstone's speech was interrupted by applause. When he could be heard, he concluded, "We will not be moved. You can't do it to us. You won't do it to us. And we will not leave this church." As he sat down, the applause was reportedly thunderous.

In April 2019, the Judicial Council ruled that the essence of the Traditional Plan was constitutional. The kernel of the legislation adopted by the 2019 General Conference becomes the ecclesiastical law of The United Methodist Church on January 1, 2020. The Judicial Council also ruled constitutional a plan and process for leaving the denomination with a modicum of amicability.

In the aftermath, resistance is unprecedented, both in verve and signatories of clergy and laity vowing ecclesiastical disobedience. Thousands in scores of Annual Conferences in The United States have signed letters of dissent and resistance. Many pastors are asking their churches to withhold conference apportionments until the 2020 General Conference, in hopes that the 2019 action will be overturned. Some of the letters are asking Boards of Ordained Ministry and bishops to refrain from any inquiry into the sexual

WHERE DO WE GO FROM HERE?

orientation of candidates seeking provisional status or ordination as Deacons or Elders. Some churches are draping LGBTQIA+ flags over the denominational identity of their church. Hundreds of churches are placing lawn signs that read either, "All are welcome here," or other words to communicate untrammeled inclusion. The Western European Churches are small in membership but outspoken in their resistance to the Traditional Plan.

To the question, "Where are we going?" the only cogent answer is that no one knows. The passage of the Traditional Plan might well reflect a survey in January 2019 done by UMNews. That indicated that about 44 percent of United Methodists consider themselves to be "conservative" or "moderate." Only about 20 percent indicated that they are theologically "liberal." Though there is no empirical data regarding the position of clergy, there is high likelihood that UMC clergy in the United States are more progressive, perhaps dramatically so, than are the laity.

*"Delegates from former Soviet Union nations and the Philippines spoke similarly. Culture in all three continents is influenced by Islamic prohibition of homosexual lifestyles."*

Bishop Michael Coyner has wisely called attention to the upcoming election of clergy and lay delegates to the 2020 General Conference. He has observed across his own ministry, "Our church has a history of voting 'no' to many new ideas the first time, but then later adopting them."

As the resistance movement grows with open petitions and signatures, the implication is that unless the 2020 GC reverses the results of the 2019 GC, the LGBTQIA+ supporters might leave. Supporters of the Traditional Plan are announcing plans to stay in The United Methodist Church as a "reform" movement, but that could morph into a decision to leave if the Traditional Plan's slim majority is reversed in 2020. "Where are we going" might be toward a fracturing along either cultural or theological lines. Indications are that we are headed for a "Donnybrook" General Conference in 2020, after which there will be the formation of a new denomination or denominations.

Lyle Schaller was one of the most prescient minds of both the Methodist and EUB Churches, and subsequently The United Methodist Church, during my half century "under appointment." His book, The Ice Cube Is Melting was not a question, but a statement. Decisions determine destiny. First, from 1960-2000, of the 10.7

115

million members of the Methodist and EUB churches, 402,000 died. If that trend continues through 2020, over six million that formed The United Methodist Church will be dead. Secondly, since 1956, the persons transferring from one UMC to another has diminished dramatically. Thirdly, even in 2003, intra-denominational conflict was motivating UMC members to leave. We can expect this factor to increase with the present atrophy of "catholic spirit" regarding same-gender marriages and the ordination or appointment of self-avowed, practicing homosexual clergy. Schaller advised intentional revitalization of churches with older membership or changing community context, but he was not optimistic about results. The "elephant in the room" is that UMC professions of faith is abominably low. This is the major contrast between the UMC in the United States and the UMC in Africa. Our American theological dividedness and our lack of acumen for bringing persons to Jesus Christ as Savior and Lord was on his radar screen.

The future is not ours to see, but with a loss of members from nearly eleven million in 1968 to less than seven million in 2018, the rise of the resistance movement in 2019, and probable losses in 2020, we are in denial if we do not see "the ice cube melting."

Though I hesitate to be accused of proof texting, Jesus' words as he wept over Jerusalem are heavy on my heart:

> **Jerusalem, Jerusalem, you who kill the prophets and stone those sent to you, how often I have longed to gather your children together, as a hen gathers her chicks under her wings, and you were not willing.**
>
> **Luke 13:34 (NIV)**

Or, to quote Patrick Henry, it is fickle to "cry 'peace, peace' when there is no peace." "O Lord of hosts, be with us yet."

**Don Haynes** is retired clergy from Western North Carolina. In his 46 years of active service, he was a Jurisdictional Delegate three times and a General Conference delegate twice. He was chair of the WNC Board of Ordained Ministry, Director of Conference Ministries, creator and speaker in thirty annual conferences for "Vision 2000," District Superintendent, VP of St. Paul School of Theology, and pastor of churches from small membership to 2200 members.

He is author of four books: *Reading the Bible Again and Seeing It for the First Time, On the Threshold of Grace, A Digest of Wesleyan Grace Theology,* and two volumes of *The Methodist Story,* the first of which is in print. Don is a graduate of High Point University and Duke Divinity School, with graduate work at Edinburgh, Oxford, and London.

# CHAPTER FOURTEEN
# William B. Lawrence

Wasn't That Special?

Reflections on the 2019 General Conference

Syndicated columnist Celia Rivenbark recently acknowledged that she and her husband are long time United Methodists. They have taught Sunday school for years in the same local church where they were married three decades ago. And they both watched the live-streamed Special Session of the 2019 General Conference in February. In a column that summarized the conference, she wrote, "this one's gonna leave a mark."[1] She is right, of course.

Any session of the General Conference is a big deal. It is our most comprehensive church meeting of decision-makers in the world. Like a Southern Baptist Convention, "the basic body of the church" (though to us, that is the annual conference, not the congregation) chooses the voters (though to us, they are "delegates" not "messengers"). Like a Roman Catholic synod, all of our bishops come from every continent where United Methodism has spread. We even have our own version of the World Court—the Judicial Council with nine international members, plus lay and clergy alternates—that has an important place in the proceedings. Any session of the General Conference is a meeting of the only body with full legislative authority for the whole church. It is an immense opportunity for United Methodists to show the world just how global, multi-cultural, multi-lingual, multi-genera-tional, ethnically inclusive, regionally diverse, and theologically deci-sive we are. It is a forum where we can display ourselves at our best.

Unfortunately, the 2019 Special Session of the General Conference did just the opposite. It demonstrated what a divided and divisive bunch we are. It displayed our deep distrust of one another and our deep dislike for one category of God's people. What's worse, its sole purpose was to discuss one topic. So the whole world could watch, as we appeared to demonstrate that the only thing of importance for us is to demonize homosexuality. It was tragic. It left a mark.

---

[1] "Dear Methodists, God Fearing is Not Gay Fearing," The News & Observer, Raleigh NC, March 9, 2019, p. 9A.

Forget the familiar hymn, "They'll Know We are Christians by Our Love." We managed to tell the world: *You will know we are United Methodists by what we say about homosexual persons and their practices and their presence in our midst.*

What the 2019 General Conference aggressively reinforced is that homosexual persons are welcome to attend our worship, donate money for our offerings, offer prayers in our services, display their talents for our benefit, trim our altars for the liturgical seasons, engage in our mission projects, receive our sacraments, sing our hymns, and teach some of our classes. But homosexual persons have to do all that on "our" terms. They are not permitted to bear witness to the faith as licensed or ordained ministers, and they are not permitted to take the vows of Christian marriage in our church buildings—unless they lie about their sexual identity and enter into heterosexual marriage. And, if they ask their pastor (or any other licensed, ordained, and appointed United Methodist minister) to preside at a wedding, they may put the clergywoman or clergyman at the risk of facing a church complaint, investigation, litigation, and expulsion from the ministerial office.

The 2019 General Conference let the whole world know that we say there are two kinds of people in the world—homosexuals and heterosexuals—and one of them is unwelcome in the leadership of our church, because of how they are made and whom they love. Further, the 2019 General Conference told congregations, institutions, and individual clergy who did not like it, that they could lump it—meaning, they can leave the denomination. In fact, the 2019 General Conference enacted a new church law that gave disgruntled local churches a map to the exits.

In displaying this message to the world, we distracted everyone from other Methodist involvements in personal and public salvation—health care, education, disaster recovery, addiction treatment, abolishing slavery, and other good news—that we brought through our evangelical ministries and missions. We have done great things for God's people.

But in 2019 we told the world to forget all that and recognize us for different values. We have made ourselves famous for placing homosexuals on the margins and in the shadows of the church. We told all of our current members and every prospective member that they have to go elsewhere in order to attend same-sex weddings involving their families. We said they have to tell a gay or lesbian loved one, who feels called into the ordained ministry of Jesus Christ, to find some other church, where God's voice can still be heard making such calls.

We used the biggest, most visible, most global gathering of the world's most influential United Methodist leaders to make the announcement that now defines us. We convened a Special Session of the General Conference and could have used it to bring good news to the world. But we botched the opportunity. As a result, we still have a division over homosexuality. And we have made a mess that we have to clean. Even if we could afford to hire the highest priced public relations firm that specializes in repairing damage to a reputation, it may take a generation to recover from the harm that this General Conference has done to our image.

But image is only the surface of the problem for United Methodists. Beneath the "mark" that has been left on the church by what happened in St. Louis, we have substantive matters to address. I will mention three the church has created for itself over homosexuality:

> We have abandoned our *doctrinal standards'* fundamental theological reliance upon God's grace in favor of a reliance upon law,[2]

> We have abandoned our *doctrine* that four sources are needed for discerning what it means to bear faithful witness to Jesus Christ and "that all four guidelines must be brought to bear in faithful, serious, theological conversation,"[3] and,

> We have abandoned our *mission* "to make disciples of Jesus Christ for the transformation of the world," choosing instead to accept things as they are, even if they threaten or impose injustice upon some of God's people.

## Doctrinal Standards[4]

First, we have abandoned the *doctrinal standard* by which all of our teaching, preaching, leading, and serving are to be measured—faith in God's grace. We have been careless about our Wesleyan theology for much too long. Now our failures have caught up with us in this crisis over homosexuality. Our doctrinal standards measure the veracity and validity of everything we teach and do. One standard is that salvation is by grace alone. We have a relationship with God solely because God extends love toward us, not because we are good enough to earn the right to enjoy such a relationship. We invented a phrase in 1972 for our Social Principles, and we declared homosex-

---

[2] See Articles VIII, IX, and X in the Articles of Religion, *The Book of Discipline of The United Methodist Church* 2016 ¶ 104, pages 67-68.

[3] See "Our Theological Task" of *The Book of Discipline of The United Methodist Church 2016* ¶ 105, page 83.

[4] *The Book of Discipline of The United Methodist Church 2016* ¶ 104 (NB: Only the Articles of Religion and the Confession of Faith are Protected Doctrinal Standards under the Restrictive Rules of the Constitution).

uality "incompatible with Christian teaching." In 1996 we put those words into a law that we have reiterated and reinforced ever since. We abandoned grace and shifted to legalism.

The words "Christian teaching" may sound authoritative, but they are undefined by the General Conference and vague in their meaning. Many things qualify as "Christian teaching." Roman Catholics and Southern Baptists agree that "Christian teaching" limits ordained ministry to men. Mennonites insist that "Christian teaching" mandates non-violence. Pentecostals assign the centrality of "Christian teaching" to speaking in tongues. Some "Christian teaching" focuses on a few passages of the Bible that condemn homosexual practices.[5] Other "Christian teaching" focuses on the remaining 900 pages of scripture that never mention it.

Inventing the term "incompatible with Christian teaching" and applying it to one specific form of human activity or identity did not mean United Methodists were more correct. It just made us more confused. To assert that something is "Christian teaching," without measuring it against our established standards of doctrine, is contrary to the foundations of our faith.

In 1972, when The United Methodist Church began to express a denominational view of homosexuality, we were consistent with the Wesleyan conviction that we cooperate with grace by accepting God's justifying mercy and by embracing God's sanctifying power to transform. We emphasized education and exhortation. We put the statement in our Social Principles, as a guide for spiritual formation in disciplined Christian living. We did not make it a church law.

In the ensuing years, the General Conference hardened our words on homosexuality. More problematically, we moved our sharply worded statements into church legislation. The process culminated when the 1996 General Conference enacted a law based on an assumption ("Since the practice of homosexuality is incompatible with Christian teaching...") and banned homosexuals from serving as ministers.[6] That 1996 General Conference enacted another law, which said "any practices declared by The United Methodist Church to be incompatible with Christian teachings" can be considered a "chargeable offense." (Of course, only one "practice" has been given that label!) Later, the 2004 General Conference revised the law. Now it says merely "being a self-avowed practicing homosexual" is a chargeable offense that can be the

---

[5] See Leviticus 18:22, 20:13, and Romans 1:27. Other texts (e.g., I Corinthians 6:9 and I Timothy 1:10) are not clear, explicit condemnations of homosexual acts, though they do condemn various forms of immorality.

[6] *The Book of Discipline of The United Methodist Church 1996* ¶ 304.3, page 172.

basis of a complaint against a minister. In effect, we United Methodists have abandoned the doctrinal standard of grace, shifted to an undefined legal standard we called "Christian teaching," found homosexuality to be "incompatible with Christian teaching," and only needed a simple majority of General Conference votes to keep saying so.

Relying on God's grace to show us mercy, offer forgiveness, and form us as Christian disciples is our doctrinal standard. But, most aggressively with the 1996 General Conference, we began insisting that the only way for the church to be delivered from the power of sin was to designate a category of human beings as sinful and then to write as well as enforce church laws that ban their sinfulness. We are now at the point where *The Book of Discipline* has a law that declares "being" a homosexual is a chargeable offense for clergy. We have, through legislation, said that only the law—not grace—can save us. This is a devastating theological failure on our part. We should confess it, not reiterate it. We should repeal such laws, not reinforce them.

## Doctrine[7]

Second, as the debate during the 2019 Special Session of the General Conference clearly demonstrated, we have abandoned our officially stated doctrine that there are four sources and guidelines to determine theologically what it means to be faithful followers of Jesus Christ. In speech after speech from the floor of the 2019 General Conference, the assertion echoed that scripture and tradition require us to reiterate and reinforce our laws opposing homosexuality.

Yet our doctrine mandates that we keep in mind "the sources from which we derive our theological affirmations and the criteria by which we assess the adequacy of our understanding and witness." Our doctrine teaches that four guidelines—scripture, tradition, experience, and reason—are to be used in "faithful, serious, theological conversation." Our doctrine says that scripture "occupies a place of primary authority among these theological sources." But our doctrine insists that, "theological reflection may also find its point of departure in tradition, experience, or rational analysis."

So we need to be clear that the word "primary" can indicate an initial level of contact or understanding without being the only level of authority. It is in "primary" school, where our first and foundational acquaintances with reading, math, art, and music begin. But we move beyond a primary level as we pursue deeper understand-

---

[7] "Our Theological Task," *The Book of Discipline of The United Methodist Church 2016* ¶ 105, pages 82-91.

ings, so we can read essays and poetry, use algebra and calculus, contrast the paintings of Degas with those of Dali, or distinguish the rhapsody of George Gershwin from the rap of Lin Manuel Miranda. The Bible is foundational, formative, and finished. It is the primary place to start. However, as Calvin said, reading it requires "spectacles." They make a text clearer than a primary reading of it.

Finding a verse somewhere in the Bible might be a place where theological reflection can begin, but it is not where our doctrine ends. Nevertheless, during the 2019 General Conference Special Session, United Methodists continued our relentless journey to abandon our own doctrine in favor of a narrow theological method by which one way of reading scripture and one approach to tradition alone supported retention of existing church law.

Our doctrine and disciplines emphasize that we receive God's loving mercy through many means of grace, all of which we should continue to use. Studying scriptures, meeting in a conference together, receiving Holy Communion, and praying are examples. But we have let the means of grace atrophy, while we have resorted to law and merit as the authorities for ecclesial decisions. We have let the General Conference set aside reason, experience, and the developing body of Christian tradition—along with a careful reading of scripture—as sources for theological clarity on all matters, including homosexuality.

Many delegates view the General Conference in a way that emphasizes the raw political power to marshal a majority that will enact a law. That way, it will only take half of the delegates plus one to enforce one's perspectives about the Bible and Christian tradition on the entire body.

Then, a simple majority can block a doctrinal obligation to use all four of the sources and guidelines for hearing God's prophetic word and receiving God's spiritual power. If legislating for the church means lining up votes rather than listening for the Lord, we are not in conference with God. Rather, we are abandoning grace in favor of our own ideas, ingenuity, opinions, and laws. And that is a substitution of some other teaching for our United Methodist doctrine.

Approaching a General Conference without a readiness to listen for a prophetic word that corrects our own views is refusing to be a recipient of God's grace. Having talked with delegates who favored the One Church Plan, the Traditional Plan, and the Connectional Conference Plan, I know that their approaches were focused on finding votes, measuring whip counts, persuading uncommitted voters, influencing leaders of delegations, and seeking other means to win. I also talked with delegates who said that they were going to read all the documents and wait for the Holy Spirit to guide them, as if pious inaction were the same as responsible discipleship. I never heard any delegates say, "I have read all the documents, I have reached my conclusion, and now I am going to find United Methodists who disagree with me so I can learn from them."

We are abandoning the means of grace that listening provides. We distrust voices that disagree with our predispositions and biases. We are less open to the possibility that those with whom we differ might offer some grace from the Lord.

Consider what happened in the regular session of the General Conference in 2016. The delegates asked the Council of Bishops for help in their legislative stalemate regarding the issues involving homosexuality. The bishops brought a proposal to defer any discussion of the topic, let the bishops name members of a commission to examine all of the laws in the *Discipline* about homosexuality, and await the report. But, having asked for a recommendation from the bishops, the delegates barely listened. Their vote to accept the proposal was a skimpy majority of 51%.

Then consider what happened when the Commission on a Way Forward produced three plans. It was a peculiar conclusion for the commission to reach. The 32 members had met many times during fifteen months. If they could not listen to each other and agree on a single approach to recommend, one can scarcely imagine how 864 delegates meeting for three days could find one best outcome. An overwhelming majority of the bishops favored the so-called One Church Plan, but an underwhelming minority of General Conference delegates listened to the bishops.

Lack of listening to one another is distrust in the grace of Christian conferencing. Lack of listening to all four sources and guidelines in "faithful, serious, theological consideration" shows distrust in our methods for defining doctrine. Lack of learning from our doctrine leads us astray.

Among the ironies in all of this is the insistence that a few *disputed* texts of scripture regarding homosexuality must be enforced as church law, when we do not insist on writing or obeying laws on matters for which there are clear Biblical mandates. In a rush toward legalism about homosexuality, we resist legalism about money, even though Jesus and the early church had plenty to say about it.[8] We are not legalistic about the requirement that a bishop have only one marriage partner.[9] We are not legalistic about letting

---

[8] Matthew 19:31; Luke 12:15; I Timothy 6:17ff; Acts 2:45

[9] I Timothy 3:2.

women lead the church, despite the Biblical word.[10] No delegate said that the General Conference broke a Biblical precept as its Committee on Presiding Officers selected Bishop Cynthia Fierro Harvey to preside at the last legislative portion of the conference. Nobody complained that she shattered scriptures, which assert women "are not allowed to speak" and "should remain silent in the churches."[11] She wore a brooch on her lapel and pearls.[12] But nobody objected to her gender or her jewelry.

Apparently, United Methodists have found ways beyond a narrow reading of the Bible on almost every topic except homosexuality, even when the clear words of texts are contrary to our customs. We were hardly pioneers in allowing women to occupy positions of leadership. Great preachers, like Phoebe Palmer in the 19th century, were excluded from ordination. The Methodist Church did not recognize that women should have full clergy rights to be conference members, travelling preachers, or itinerant elders until 1956. The United Methodist Church did not elect a woman to the office of Bishop until 1980.[13] But with clear spectacles and proper guidance from experience, reason, and the developing Christian tradition, we have shown doctrinally that we can read the Bible as a text of grace, not as a pretext for writing enforceable laws—except for one topic. On homosexuality, we have gone into graceless legalism.

## Mission[14]

Third, we have abandoned our mission. When an immigrant named Francis Asbury arrived in North America, he brought with him the understanding of the Methodist mission on which John Wesley had sent him—to reform the continent and spread scriptural holiness over the land. That mission statement has had various formulations through the centuries. The current one talks about making disciples of Jesus Christ for the transformation of the world. The important point is that Methodism—including The United Methodist Church today—is on a mission that is dedicated not solely to transforming individual souls but also to transforming societal systems.

---

[10] I Corinthians 14:35-36 .

[11] I Corinthians 14:34 (NIV).

[12] I Peter 3:3.

[13] All of the Jurisdictional Conferences in the United States have elected women to the Episcopacy, but most of the Central Conferences have not yet elected a woman to the office of Bishop.

[14] *The Book of Discipline of The United Methodist Church 2016* ¶ 120, page 93.

The fact that The United Methodist Church is now a global body, not a narrowly North American one, does not alter the Wesleyan mission. It means that United Methodists on every continent share in the commitment that we are sent to transform souls and societies.

In the weeks prior to the 2019 General Conference, I know that delegates from various annual conferences struggled with a conundrum in our global church. In the United States, it is now indisputable that homosexual couples have the same constitutional right to be married as heterosexual couples do.[15] In other countries where The United Methodist Church is present, the laws differ widely. In Germany, same-sex marriage is legal.[16] In Russia, same-sex marriage is not recognized, but it is not criminalized. In Nigeria, not only is homosexual marriage illegal, but also homosexual activity is a criminal offense. In places where United Methodists live and love and serve, homosexual practices are capital crimes. On occasion, General Conference delegates have argued that they cannot vote to remove our church laws that prohibit homosexuality since their home countries outlaw homosexuality. To perform a wedding for a same-sex couple cannot be permitted in the church because it is not permitted in the country, the arguments say.

Once again, people called Methodists have to confront a missional crisis. Given our first mission to reform continents and spread scriptural holiness—or, in another formulation, to make disciples of Jesus Christ for the transformation of the world—we are to transform the unjust and unloving policies of nations, rather than surrender to them.

Not long ago, in parts of the United States, there were laws banning interracial marriage. Those laws would have prohibited any minister in our denomination from performing interracial marriage ceremonies. In addition, other segregationist and racist laws in sections of the United States prevented African-Americans from voting, from living in certain neighborhoods, from attending certain schools, and from acquiring certain jobs, based solely on race. Followers of the Wesleyan mission could have simply surrendered and succumbed to such state laws.

However, many American Methodists embraced our historic mission to transform the world and made countless sacrifices to alter unjust laws. People who opposed racist laws and segregated systems faced threats, beatings, arson, and lynching when they protested. People who marched against those laws were jailed, berated, harmed,

---

[15] The Supreme Court of the United States, Obergefell v. Hodges, June 26, 2015.

[16] Same-sex partnerships were recognized in 2001, and same-sex marriage became legal in 2017.

and killed. A white Methodist minister in Birmingham, Alabama, who prophetically addressed the evils of segregation in his Sunday sermons, had to endure the verbal tirades and torment hurled at him from the pews by one of his own parishioners—Bull Connor, the public safety commissioner for Birmingham and the person who authorized some horrific violence against those who sought an end to racist laws, was in fact a Methodist.[17]

If there are laws, cultural practices, and social patterns that violate the gospel in areas of the world where United Methodism is present, it is our mission to reform those continents and transform those public orders. We cannot limit our witness in the name of Jesus Christ to those places and situations where the law allows us to do so.

## Conclusion

So the General Conference in 2019 did more than reiterate and reinforce existing church laws regarding homosexuality. It distanced us from our doctrinal standards, our doctrine, and our mission. It damaged our image in the world, to be sure. And it exposed our faults and failures to be faithful.

On April 26, 2019, in response to the special General Conference actions, the Judicial Council issued two decisions, and the divisive denominational dilemma deepened. Decision 1378 gave constitutional approval to laws opposing homosexuality as the defining center of United Methodist authority and power. Decision 1379 cleared the way for a local church, feeling unhappy about this, to leave the denomination.

We have made a mess. Now we have to clean it. And, in the process, we have to make plenty of room available for all of God's people—regardless of their sexual identity—into the full life and leadership of the church.

**William B. Lawrence** is Professor Emeritus of American Church History at Perkins School of Theology, Southern Methodist University, and an ordained elder in The United Methodist Church in the the North Texas Annual Conference. A native of Wilkes-Barre, Pennsylvania, he received his BA degree in Religion, with Distinction, from Duke University, his M. Div. from Union Theological Seminary in New York, and a Ph. D. in Homiletics and Historical Theology, with Distinction, from Drew University. He also holds an honorary Doctor of Divinity degree from LaGrange College and is a Research Fellow in The Center for Studies in the Wesleyan Tradition at Duke Divinity School.

---

[17] William E. Nicholas, *Go and Be Reconciled: Alabama Methodists Confront Racial Injustice,* 1954-1974 (Montgomery: New South Books, 2018), pages 16-17, 48.

# CHAPTER FIFTEEN
# Bishop Sharma D. Lewis
Where Do We Go From Here?
That's the Million-Dollar Question

Where do we go from here? It is the million-dollar question on the hearts and minds of clergy and laity in The United Methodist Church as we go forward and anticipate the 2020 General Conference.

I watched the 2019 Special General Conference for four days with anticipation and hope for the future of The United Methodist Church. I was so bold to believe that maybe a "miracle" could happen on the Special General Conference floor that would unite us to be the body of Christ called Methodist.

> *"I watched the deep pain that was articulated from many delegates, the tears that trickled down the cheeks, and the anger that human sexuality is still the prominent issue that divides our church.*

To my utter dismay that didn't happen. Instead, I watched the deep pain that was articulated from many delegates, the tears that trickled down the cheeks, and the anger that human sexuality is still the prominent issue that divides our church.

I have come to realize that human sexuality is a topic that the body of Christ will never agree upon. In watching our Special General Conference, I saw lines being drawn in the sand. I watched as people quoted scripture to argue for stronger wording in the *Book of Discipline.* While at the same time, people were in tears, crushed by the continual feeling of rejection and exclusion from their faith community. I affirm that ALL people are valued and of sacred worth. To the sisters and brothers of the LGBTQIA+ community, know that you are loved and wanted in our local churches. I want to affirm the evangelical community that often times feel their beliefs are misunderstood and perceived as being driven by animosity, instead of their deep abiding faith in Jesus Christ, and a quest to follow in His footsteps.

Yet, the question still stands. Where do we go from here?

I want to assure the reader that I desire and believe as a consecrated United Methodist Bishop to lead the whole church in claiming its mission in making disciples of Jesus Christ for the transformation of the world (*2016 Book of Discipline*, ¶403). I believe in my heart that people need to have a personal relationship with Jesus Christ. I believe that if our church could focus and pursue the mission of The United Methodist Church, we may realize that we have more things in common than differences, no matter what our theological convictions may be.

> *"My prayer is that we end the harm that we have inflicted on one another and pursue our mission of The Methodist Church."*

According to *The Great Commission Guide[1]*, it is reported that more than two billion people have never heard the message of salvation being given to all people when Jesus died for our sins. As reported by this report, they haven't had the chance to accept or reject the love of Jesus Christ. As believers, we have the responsibility to share the love, forgiveness, and grace of Jesus Christ. If we do truly believe in the love and healing power of Jesus Christ, are we willing to tear ourselves apart and stray from the course He laid out for us?

Have we in The United Methodist Church decided that human sexuality is the only topic in the church that needs healing? Have we become a one topic issue in our denomination? If we are honest with each other, we see we have much work to do in the Kingdom of God.

In 2019, we are still plagued with racism, sexism, misogyny, sexual misconduct, women's inequality, immigration, ever increasing black male incarceration, an opioid epidemic, churches not accepting people of color, and resisting female leadership, to just name a few areas that require our attention and healing. My prayer is that we end the harm that we have inflicted on one another and pursue our mission of The Methodist Church.

This is not a time to run and hide. It is a time for us to stand strong and courageous like Joshua, to show and witness the love of

---

[1] https://alliancefortheunreached.org/wp-content/uploads/2018/04/Great-Commission-Action-Guide-04-18.pdf

Jesus Christ. Let us pray for our Church's mission to come alive again! Matthew 28:19-20 states:

> ... **therefore go and make disciples of all nations,**
> **baptizing them in the name of the Father and**
> **of the Son and of the Holy Spirit,**
> **and teaching them to obey everything**
> **I have commanded you. And surely I am with you**
> **always, to the very end of the age.**
>
> **Matthew 28:19-20 (NIV)**

The work we do as The United Methodist Church is vital and life-giving. Though our hearts are bruised and our souls have been affected by this Special General Conference, we remain the church. We still have a mission, and they are so many hearts and lives that can be transformed through the work of God. Let us work together as one. Let us turn to God in these unsettling times. Let us encourage one another and allow the Holy Spirit to guide us.

**Bishop Sharma D. Lewis,** resident bishop of the Richmond episcopal area, became the first African-American woman to be elected bishop in the Southeastern Jurisdiction of The United Methodist Church in 2016.

Prior to her episcopal assignment, she held a distinguished record of service in the North Georgia Conference including her appointment as district superintendent of the Atlanta-Decatur-Oxford District in 2010. In 2007, Bishop Lewis' remarkable pastoral leadership at Wesley Chapel, a three-year tenure, led to over 600 new and restored members and worship attendance doubled. She received the Harry Denman Award for Evangelism in 2010 as well as the G. Ross Freeman Leadership Award.

# CHAPTER SIXTEEN
# Laquaan Malachi
Going Back To The Future Is Not An Option

Time does not allow us to go backwards. Whether we like it or not, we can only go forward. After the catastrophe that was General Conference 2019, I seriously considered turning in my credentials. As you might imagine, it was a heavy thought to bear.

The United Methodist Church is the only church I have ever loved. It's also the only church that has ever made me feel loved. Even so, I cannot abide when I see harmful, dangerous policies. What happened in St. Louis broke my heart in ways I didn't know were possible.

Like me, there are many United Methodists who find themselves feeling left out in the cold. Many Methodist have opened their eyes for the very first time to the sin we have been complicit in. I pray that this experience grows us into something better than we are now.

I fell in love with The United Methodist Church in my early twenties through my Wesley Foundation. My faith journey has been a winding road with many traumatic experiences. I am a twenty-eight-year-old Black man, raised in South Carolina as a church-going Baptist. The strip of South Carolina I grew up in was referred by the federal government as The Corridor of Shame. I have seen first-hand what happens to people who grow up in places like The Corridor.

I now live and pastor in North Minneapolis, a part of the city that has been historically divested, deliberately underfunded, and consistently underserved. It's the Blackest part of Minneapolis. It surprises a lot of people to learn that, while Minnesota ranks as one of the best states to live in for White people, many studies have proclaimed Minnesota as the worst state in the nation for Black people. I've learned lessons I wish no one had to learn.

It breaks my heart to know that my church, which was there for me when I needed it most, was simultaneously the agent of great harm to others. I know from my own experience that harmful experiences in church can have devastating and lasting effects on people.

Frankly, unless something changes soon, I'm afraid the future of my church is bleak. Either we undergo some miraculous progressive reform, or we continue to be a church that not only sanctions, but encourages, harm. Even with reform, our public witness has been indelibly stained. There is no easy way forward for The United Methodist Church. If it still exists in a few years, its strength and witness will likely be greatly diminished. Now that we have faltered in our ability to fully welcome LGBTQIA+ people, we must be steadfast in our proclamation of their sacredness as we move forward.

As we consider the future, LGBTQIA+ should be our central concern, not an occasional afterthought. We have a long way to go to if we are ever to rebuild the trust we have lost. LGBTQIA+ Methodists have long been betrayed, and we are repeating mistakes that we have made before.

Our current predicament is eerily similar to our contentious history with racism. There are lessons to be learned about how poorly the UMC has dealt with its legacy of racism. There are separate Methodist denominations that exist because Black people were driven from traditional Methodism.

This is a problem we have had since our earliest days in America. The sin of racism split our denomination as a precursor to it splitting the nation. Even after we acknowledged our failure, we again put our racism on full display. Compromise is not always a good and noble thing. Sometimes, to compromise is to betray those at the bottom of the power dynamic. When we allowed members and pastors to own people, we were compromising. It was a compromise that lead to the establishment of Central Conferences in the 1968 merger.

It seems to me that we are now repeating the mistakes of our past. Even the One Church Plan, which was broadly popular, was still an immoral compromise that put all the burden on LGBQTIA+ members. Compromise at the expense of the marginalized is immoral and, in my way of thinking, unacceptable.

My call is remembering the people. Particularly the very people we have harmed the most. In the midst of meetings and conferences related to this issue, this sentiment always seems to be lost. I hear people talking about pensions and institutions, but not so much about people.

I understand the need to be thorough. I also understand most of us are in the conversation with good intentions. Still, we must be careful to remain steadfast in our focus to do no harm, because we have done enough of that already. What we have done in the past is irreversible. Not only have we managed to trample an entire class of people, but we have done so while also proclaiming the name of Christ. We have caused irreparable harm.

Centering marginalized voices means more than just consulting those who don't look like ourselves. Centering their voices is not the same as using their voices. As a Black pastor in Minnesota, I am wary of those who want my face, or to be more specific, my skin. My skin can be used to make photos, brochures, and leadership look "diverse."

> *"We should take heed to not repeat past mistakes, often made in traditional spaces, treating marginalized experiences as an afterthought."*

Centering marginalized voices means more than just passing them the microphone, its more akin to letting them build the platform. Marginalized people are the very people Jesus calls us to serve and be among. Their oppression has given them the gift of recognizing who is being left out.

We should take heed to not repeat past mistakes, often made in traditional spaces, treating marginalized experiences as an afterthought. If we want marginalized identities to feel welcome in whatever comes next, we must give them real power instead of lip service.

The marginalized are accustomed to living in a world that isn't built for them, so they might have a few good ideas about how to build a better world. Leaders must learn to consider the ideas of everyone, as opposed to falling into defensive behaviors.

Institutions often love diversity, as long as diversity doesn't rock the boat. Every child of God deserves to be valued and must have a role in shaping the dominant discourse, or Methodism in America will continue to fall short of what it is called to be.

Centering marginalized voices doesn't balance the scales of our injustice, but it is a firm step in the right direction. Racism has always been our great silent sin and homophobia seems a natural extension of that. The Methodist Church in its various forms has been too quick to ally itself with institutional and systemic sin. Many clergy and members have sacrificed so much of themselves to remain a part of our body. They have paid untold and uncountable costs. Whatever we do next, their voices must be a central part of it.

To do otherwise would be to betray them once again.

Let's not forget how we got here. It is our own institutional sin that has brought us to this place and now we must bear the consequences. It seems that we never learned our lesson. Making mistakes is human. But when we intentionally overlook the ways in which our systems cause harm, then we are complicit in that very harm. Our collective apathy in exchange for stability is not a wise trade-off.

> *"We are being presented with a golden opportunity to dream boldly. We must resist the urge to cower into the comfort of the status quo."*

With the steadily climbing rate of suicide among LGBTQIA+, our decisions have real, human costs. As I write this chapter, there is a story across my screen of a gay teenage boy who just committed suicide. Our refusal to boldly and openly support and accept those with different lifestyles than our own is a part of what contributes to the hopelessness these youth often feel. A "One Church style" plan is no longer feasible. The spirit of that immoral compromise died with the vote at General Conference. Only true justice is acceptable at a bare minimum. Some things are not to be compromised.

Whatever the future of Methodism turns out to be, we must focus on people. Loving our neighbors is the foundation on which Methodism in America was built. GC2019 showed us that the incivility of the political realm has made its way into the church. When LGBTQIA+ protestors were thrown out into the streets at General Conference, we displayed our sin and hardheartedness before the world. We can't undo what has already been done.

We are being presented with a golden opportunity to dream boldly. We must resist the urge to cower into the comfort of the status quo. My fear is that in our zeal to restore our image and provide stability for our clergy and congregants, we are setting the bar too low. We can do better than UMC 2.0; a half step to the left. We have an opportunity to build something that is just and equitable. Now is the time to be revolutionary. People will say that broad and sweeping change in this particular moment is unfeasible. They are wrong. Who knows if we will ever have such an opportunity again? We stand not only by our own two feet, but also on the presiding guidance of God. Uncertainty is not the enemy, and we need to trust God to guide us.

The days of generic top-down leadership are over. We must allow for greater flexibility on the local level so that ministry can be shaped to best fit its context. We must resist the urge to buy into systems that were created centuries ago for a world that no longer exists. It is time to reimagine what Methodism in today's world can look like. It's time for us to get off the fence. The idea of a great "Methodist Middle" has been a failure. Justice should not be debatable.

If we are dying, we are dying of self-inflicted wounds. I stand for the full inclusion of everyone in our church. If what remains of Methodism has any backbone, this is where they will stand, too. The only place to go from here is forward.

**Pastor Laquaan Malachi** is a licensed local pastor in the Minnesota Annual Conference of the United Methodist Church. He was born and raised in Bennettsville, South Carolina but he currently resides in Minneapolis. He attended undergrad at Francis Marion University and seminary at Candler School of Theology. He has a passion for people and justice. Pastor Malachi is also a spoken word artist whose work often includes themes surrounding justice and/or mental health.

1936 General Conference held in Columbus, Ohio.

# CHAPTER SEVENTEEN
# M. Douglas Meeks

The United Methodist Church:
Coming to Our Theological Senses

If anyone doubted that The United Methodist Church is in crisis, the debacle of the special 2019 General Conference should have removed any question about that. Sad to say, the General Conference, as expensive as it was in time and money, did nothing to end the crisis. Those who backed the One Church Plan are in despair and tempted to leave the church just as those who supported the Traditional Plan would have done had they "lost." But this is not the time to leave the church. It is rather a time to become steadfastly present and vocal. Whatever happens in the follow-up, this special General Conference signaled a time of significant change in the UMC.

Schism, breaking the Body of Jesus Christ, is never the answer. Schism is sinful; there is nothing heroic about it. If we could step back far enough, we would be ashamed of our playground banter daring the other side to drop out of the church and leave the ground to us. United Methodism has always been part of the modern church uniting movement, but our union has always been fragile, requiring patience and forbearance. Indeed, our union has been fragile ever since the first conference, the Christmas Conference of 1784, when our new church was called into being. It took only a moment before we decided to reject Wesley's declaration that one could not be a Methodist while owning slaves. Not long after we split over slavery in 1844 and shamefully provided our nation with a justification for a profoundly violent split over the economy of slavery. Consequently, American Methodism has suffered the deep wounds of failed reconstruction, Jim Crow, and systemic racism. We learned to shape our theology to be in accord with "unalterable" economy and embedded racism. Our theology, we assumed, had to make allowance for what could not be changed. We have argued over bishops, authority of scripture, form of governance, apportionments, style of worship, and the meaning of the Great Commission (Matt 28), and in each case never without the shadow of our divisions having their sway.

137

Are we to repeat this history by conjuring theologies that conform to various views of homosexuality? Once we spilt over slavery; now, supposedly, we are splitting over homosexuality. I say "supposedly" because the issues are much deeper than homosexuality. If we could let dissolve the fog from our confusion about sexuality, we could see that the church of Jesus Christ should be daily struggling with issues facing our nation and the world: poverty, racial hatred, the degradation of nature, health care, and the plethora of human rights that are under siege. These issues are so difficult it seems we would prefer to stick with homosexuality.

The first step toward union, now as always, is confessing our sin, the sin that has led to this crisis of division. That sin, at least in large part, is our misplaced trust in the invincibility of Methodist bigness and Methodist polity. Our sin is trusting implicitly in our bureaucracy, our "connection," and our "democracy" to solve problems that can only be addressed by our baptismal reality before God. Denominational purity defined according to our lights, based on a "law book" that grows too heavy by accretion every four years, can easily become heresy. Heresy, simply put, is the displacement of the lordship of Jesus Christ by our own criterion of truth.

In this time of crisis, we would do well to remember the most important Christian confession of the twentieth century, the Barmen Declaration (1934). It was written out of the crisis brought on by the capture of all institutions, including the church, by Nazism. The Declaration defined the real problem for the church as the loss of its being: Jesus Christ in the Triune God. This loss meant that the *status confessionis* was in effect, that is, the necessity of the church to stand up and confess its Lord, the one act on which the truth of everything else in the church depends.

In the midst of this crisis we would also do well to turn to John Wesley's sermon "Catholic Spirit." Wesley held to the dictum "In Essentials Unity, In Non-Essentials Liberty, In All Things Charity" which first appeared in a Lutheran tract during the Thirty-Years War (1618–1648), a time of bloody conflict fueled by religious differences. For Wesley, union required the distinction between "essentials" of the faith and "opinions." Utterly realistic, Wesley recognized that "several people will be of several minds" and a "variety of opinions necessarily implies a variety of practice."[1] Since the church is full of human beings, Wesley thought we should not be surprised

---

[1] Quotes are from Wesley's sermon "Catholic Spirit," in *John Wesley's Sermons: An Anthology*, ed. Albert C. Outler and Richard P. Heitzenrater (Nashville: Abingdon Press, 1991), 300-309.

to find "invincible ignorance" and, furthermore, we should go no further than its lodging in ourselves to recognize it. "To be ignorant of many things, and to mistake in some, is the necessary condition of humanity." The church, like all human institutions, suffers from "invincible prejudice which is often so fixed in tender minds that it is afterwards impossible to tear up what has taken so deep a root."

This goes for the whole spectrum of minds and hearts in the church, from right to left. Thus, Wesley thought that within our union in Christ, the importance of conscience was simply a recognition of our humanity. "Everyone must follow the dictates of his (or her) own conscience in simplicity and godly sincerity. He (or she) must be fully persuaded in his (or her) own mind, and then act accordingly to the best light he (or she) has."

To be sure, Wesley was a person of opinions. He knew even church people were not going to be without their opinions, and some opinions are good and worthwhile and should not be held in silence. But opinions divide and must be examined in clear view of essentials. Christian unity requires adherence to the essential core of Christian beliefs while we endure quarrels about "opinions." The question, for Wesley, is finding the way essentials should govern opinions.

## General Conference

We can be thankful for all the hard work of the Commission on the Way Forward and of those who prepared for the General Conference and carried it out while at the same time saying that three days to solve the crisis of the church is, please forgive me, a joke. In the ways we have attempted to prevent the split we have trusted what we have created and not, sorry to say, the Triune God. We have trusted our Constitution (made by us and not sacrosanct), our modes of leadership (often debated and not eternal), our built-in regionalism (a primary deterrent to our serving the kingdom of God and not a historical necessity), and our cultural nationalism (so easily exalted but not the work of God). All of these are *our* products.

As it is and has been for many years, conversation on the essentials of our faith is rudely cut short on the floor of the General Conference. There is no real conferral or conversation on the things that matter most. It is as if theology is ruled out of order. It seems out of place to speak of the core of our faith. Though it is blithely assumed, it is as if there is in fact no agreement on the Lordship of Jesus Christ; to ask what this actually means for any matter is to interrupt the agenda, to impede our search for something to make a law of, instead of what counts as true faith. Trained as we are by our public politics, we study the stratagems that will tilt votes toward our opinion. We have a blind faith in democracy. But a vote does not decide the truth. Democracy is a form of government only for people who are willing to keep working together in search of the truth after votes are recorded. Whatever the outcome of the present crisis, the General Conference has to be rethought, perhaps reinvented. We can no longer expect a highly politicized gathering every four years to sort out the essentials and the opinions.

Living in the truth that is Jesus Christ in the Spirit requires something like what Acts 15 describes as the first Christian council, a sustained deliberation that ends "for it has seemed good to the Holy Spirit and to us." This is what Wesley had in mind with "conference" as a mode of life and a mode of governance: being in council with one another. The future of United Methodism, then, will have to re-invent forms of *conciliarism*, a well-tested way of living though crises in the history of the church, a version of which gave rise to Methodism.

But it will have to be a conciliarism that is focused in the congregation and the local community. So, we will have to practice again another well-worn ecclesial concept: *subsidiarity*, the conviction that all important decisions should be made as close to the local community as possible. As a church we have been so agitated by the fear of opting for a congregationalist polity that we miss the extreme importance Wesley placed in the congregation and the cluster of congregations. Conference is a form of conciliarism, but conference has to take place first in the congregation, or conferencing at higher levels will inevitably falter. The congregation is where the essentials and opinions have to be worked out in sustained conversation, conferencing. This means, I believe, that the health and integrity of General Conference depends on and begins with the health and integrity of the Quarterly Conference and all other gatherings in the local congregation and clusters of congregations. Where else will our church learn to do theology as the search for the essentials?

The dispute concerning homosexuality, like all ethical issues facing humanity, has to be seen in the light of the essential core of our faith. Like General Conference, many pastors assume that the essential core of faith is settled and does not need to trouble the waters; we can proceed immediately to morals. But it is not settled. The reason we send persons to seminary is that they will be able to lead the congregation precisely in bringing the essential core of our faith into conversation with issues like homosexuality. Is it possible that schools of theology have become so focused on cognitive methods and scholarly disciplines that we have not provided the space in which persons can gain the courage to say and live the gospel in the congregation planted in the world?

For a moment, imagine, if you will, that General Conference, indeed our whole governing system, were not based on the U. S. federal government. Then we might see more clearly that our Connection is not what we thought it was. Could our Connection and General Conference be viewed in terms conciliarism and subsidiarity rather than an abstract system separated from people in the congregation? Thinking from bottom up about how the church is governed, we will have to reinvent the District. This will require a new culture rising from the Lord's Table that eschews competition among pastors and congregations. This is precisely the reason for the existence of the District, that is, the good health of the common life and mission of the congregations in a region. If conciliarism and subsidiarity are not practiced in the congregation and district, they will never be practiced anywhere. And we will be left to stew in our own juices as we continue fruitlessly to shuffle our organizational furniture.

## Scripture

What have we put in the place of the lordship of Jesus Christ as regards the issue of homosexuality? What prevents the ordination or entering onto marriage of homosexuals? Though the authority of the Bible is often mentioned, it is primarily natural law and social custom that for some in the church continue to support the bans against homosexuals. Natural law and social injunction should be taken seriously and respectfully, but they are not the Scripture. They are not the will of God in Jesus Christ. A church that established itself on the denial of the full humanity of homosexuals would indeed be on shaky grounds. The essentials of the faith would call such a church into question.

In moments of recess from bureaucratic squabbling we do bring the Bible into the picture, but we do so by employing one or another modern theory of biblical interpretation (literal reading and exis-tentialist, non-eschatological interpretation seem to be favorites on the fringes of our denomination) in place of Jesus Christ. The one extreme eclipses the life, death, and resurrection of Jesus and reduces the gospel to moral commands. The other extreme excludes the resurrection and the kingdom of God and leaves us to choose among secular theories of the right and the good. Our interpreta-tion becomes scripture. Our interpretation becomes the standard

141

of truth for ethical decisions. But the Bible is not the source of ideas that will reinforce how we think everyone should be and act. The Bible is not our servant, it is the servant of God. The Bible points to the living crucified resurrected Jesus who is the judge and criterion of the Bible as well as of us. If the living Christ is our judge and savior, then we have to be much more circumspect about saying that *our interpretation* of the Bible is the ultimate arbiter of truth – or, for that matter, the General Conference, bishops, pastors, professors, or lay organizations.

We stand under the Bible, not over it. As we read the Bible, the risen Lord is the judge of what we say about homosexuality, or any other question of life we face. As Wesleyans we should know that we cannot live without the Bible, for it witnesses to Jesus Christ, crucified and risen; but we dare not see the Bible as an idol that replaces Jesus and the Spirit and the One who sends them for the salvation of the world. The Bible is not our savior; the the Triune God is the redeemer of the creation.

The *essentials* are expressed in worship, but we have to be sure that the Triune God witnessed by the Scripture is the One we are worshipping. Theology is the disciplined, patient discussion that follows: Did we worship truthfully? And how would we know whether we did or not? How can we worship more faithfully the next time? Christian theology inevitably turns to the Trinity as the way of shaping our "experience." The Trinity is essential. We are all named by the Trinity in our baptism. This is what makes us indissolubly one. "Trinity" both names the living God into whose life we are baptized and the teaching by which we shape our thought about our life and work in the Triune community. The doctrine of the Trinity has sometimes become arcane and abstract, but in the first place the Trinity is our primary way of reading the Gospels. When hearing the word "Trinity," we should first think simply about the relationships between Jesus, the Holy Spirit, and the One who sends them – not about abstract metaphysical concepts.

The Trinity is our way of holding together and understanding this story of the Gospels that "authors" us. And, according to Paul, the Trinity, which shows how the three persons are related in the Gospels, shows us also how we should relate to each other in the church. For example, no person of the Trinity works alone, each has a name, but the name depends on the relation to the others, each takes initiative at different times. This describes the relations of our baptismal life in the church and is the context in which we should work out our decisions and actions in relation to everyone in the congregation and in the world, including our homosexual brothers and sisters.

## Bishops

The way out of this crisis and our future of uniting also depends on bishops. From our Methodist beginnings we have quarreled over the office of bishop. We decided to keep bishops, though our older Methodist cousins in Britain have done quite alright without them. But what's the point of having bishops if they are not learned and bold teachers of the faith, if they do not carry the burden of making certain that the essentials of the faith are taught and lived in a region? Of course, this is as difficult to do as it is for any pastor in a congregation; there is no more difficult place on earth to speak and live the gospel of Jesus Christ than in North America, so beset as our society is by a multitude of alluring gods.

We embarrassingly put bishops on the stage and administer all means of keeping them under control. The bishops we remember are the ones who have escaped this control and have said the truth in places where power corrupts the gospel. We dare not put a theological straitjacket on the conscience of bishops as they seek to lead us in discerning and living the essentials of our faith, except to say clearly and openly when they distort the essentials. As one of my old Sunday School teachers used to say, there is a slight but crucial difference between being "a fool for Christ" and a "damned fool." Is it too much to say that we want bishops who know this difference and are not afraid of appearing as fools for Christ in such a time and place as this?

Two initiatives the Council of Bishops took in recent times, one on Children and Poverty and one on God's Renewed Creation, are excellent examples of episcopal teaching. They follow what Wesley meant by "Practical Divinity;" they teach the faith precisely in relation to human suffering and struggle and not in abstraction. One wonders whether the slogan "Making disciples for the transformation of the world," even though it sounds good, is all that helpful because it gives no concrete content to discipleship and world transformation before the "God who is present among the least."

The teaching of bishops is particularly crucial as they bring the gospel to bear on the new situations of mission. If God is present in Jesus where the mission is most threatened, then it may be permissible and advisable to change rules for the sake of mission, lest the rules of the church make it moribund and incapable of the mission to which its Lord has called it. Polity follows the gospel and life lived in the worldly reign of the kingdom of God. Not the other way around.

## Sacraments

The paltry ritual practices of baptism and communion in our denomination may be at the heart of our problem. We've come to view the sacraments as rituals that belong to the church. Quite to the contrary, the sacraments of baptism and communion are God's instruments for creating the church. Without the reality of the sacraments in our lives, preaching the gospel can hardly make sense. If we are not living baptism and communion in the totality of our lives, we are not comprehending that the good news of the kingdom and Jesus is actually meant for our life decisions. Without living the promises God makes and the promises we make in baptism, we will blithely go on thinking of ourselves as a voluntary association in which whoever interprets the rules will dominate.

In this crisis it must be remembered that we are a *promised* people, a fact which rightly makes us question, however much we appreciate it, democracy as an avenue to the truth. The crisis of the church, which extends well beyond the ethical question of homosexuality, can be addressed only by our trust in the real presence of Jesus Christ. But we have to be willing to stay at the table until a decision is made that is consonant with the living Christ and seems good to the Holy Spirit and all of us. We may think we have short-circuited the need for such patience in Christ by choosing to model ourselves on the bureaucratic governance of the United States. But does anyone doubt that the executive, legislative, and judicial structure of the United States is broken and will have to be transformed in order to protect what we Americans consider most crucial: "liberty and justice for all." I believe the same is true of the UMC.

## Love, Sanctification, Revival

John Wesley's greatest contribution to the church universal is his understanding of sanctification. We American Methodists have generally been satisfied to stick with justification, whereas Wesley claimed that justification is the beginning of Christian life, not its end. Justification makes sanctification possible. Mystified as we are about sanctification, we have settled for a "justification church." We preach for justification, and after it is assumed that we are justified, there is basically nothing left but the maintenance of the church and a pure moral life. For Wesley, sanctification is nothing other than the love of God and our neighbor. All the essentials of our faith are directed toward God's love of us, our love of God, and our love of our neighbor. We cannot love God without loving the neighbor and cannot love the neighbor without loving God. Such love is extraordinarily difficult and can be accomplished only by good-willed people with the patience for extended conversation (conciliarism). People who want to prevent schism will accept God's gift of patience to discern what is true and truly essential. Therefore, we should follow Wesley in his claim that the only sure way to truth is love, including the love of those with whom we most disagree, including the love of our enemies. We are of course tempted to part with Wesley and Jesus on this because it is not realistic enough.

The present crisis has brought us up short. Our "realism" doesn't look so smart anymore. We are faced with the old ecclesial question: Is excommunication possible? Who should be excommunicated? All baptized persons should shutter at the rejection of any we might decide to exclude. The tradition generally has said the only one who should be excluded is the one who excludes others from the Table of the Lord by tests, that is, tests that themselves would assume the Lord, the Host of the meal, is not himself present. And if some would say, "we do not exclude homosexuals from the Lord's Table, we only exclude them from marriage and ordination," they deny what is essential to the faith. They hold to an opinion that a person could be a disciple of Jesus without being considered a candidate for marriage and ordination. Holding this opinion means one denies one's own flesh. At the Lord's table the whole person is present, the whole life of a person is being redeemed. To deny baptized Christians marriage and ordination simply on the basis of sexual orientation is contrary to the gospel. We don't get Jesus without the friends of Jesus. And we don't get to reject some of Jesus' friends on our own cognizance.

> *"The present crisis has brought us up short. Our 'realism' doesn't look so smart anymore."*

I certainly don't know what will transpire in the UMC in the coming months and years. What I do know is that no one who lives according to the promises of Jesus Christ and lives as one promised to Christ and who is in communion with the present Christ and the recipients of Christ's grace may be dismissed from the church or denied ordination and marriage. This moment of *status confessionis* will surely bring many surprises of conscience and of obedience to Jesus. Bold statements by the clergy and laity of the Western Jurisdiction and of several annual conferences have made clear that many in our church will simply not follow the bans against homosexuals. They will follow Luther and Wesley in practicing ecclesial disobedience, in standing up for the "essentials." "Here I stand, I can do no other." But because all essentials have their life in the love of God and neighbor, each of us has to search ourselves to see whether we have lodged the essentials in our own narrow definition of the church, leaving ourselves open to self-righteousness.

We Methodists are inveterate revivalists. Revival (*re-vivre*) means to come to life again for the gospel of Jesus and the kingdom of God. Revival will look different than what we have known in the past. But it will depend on discovering the essentials of our faith and the common confession of them. Filled with what Wesley called "the "energy of love," let us hope that God will look upon us and say: "Your builders outdo your destroyers" (Isa 49:17 NRSV).

**Douglas Meeks** is the Cal Turner Chancellor Professor of Theology and Wesleyan Studies, Emeritus, in the Divinity School of Vanderbilt University. He was formerly Dean and Professor of Systematic Theology at Wesley Theological Seminary in Washington, D.C. and before that Professor of Systematic Theology at Eden Theological Seminary, St. Louis. ·

Professor Meeks is the author or editor of 18 books, including *Origins of the Theology of Hope* (Fortress); *God the Economist, The Doctrine of God, Political Economy* (Fortress); *The Future of the Methodist Theological Traditions; What Should Methodists Teach: Wesleyan Tradition and Modern Diversity; The Portion of the Poor; Good News to the Poor in the Wesleyan Tradition, Trinity, Community and Power: Mapping Trajectories in Wesleyan Theology;* and *Wesleyan Perspectives on the New Creation.*

# CHAPTER EIGHTEEN
# Rebekah Miles

When Brothers and Sisters Fight to the Death: Ecclesiology, Mission, and the Future of The United Methodist Church

"When brothers and sisters fight to the death, a stranger inherits the father's estate."

The Igbo people of Nigeria offer wise counsel, saying, "When brothers and sisters fight to the death, a stranger inherits the father's estate." We in The United Methodist Church find ourselves in a brutal fight that is not only dangerous to all of the members of the family but to the estate itself. Whatever resentment the brothers and sisters of The United Methodist Church bear each other, they share in common a deep love for that estate. The estate is not the property. It is not the surplus funds. It is not the boards and agencies. The estate is our mission, as we contemporary United Methodists put it, to make disciples of Jesus Christ for the transformation of the world. In our fighting, we have put at risk the very thing we value the most, the thing that makes us who we are—the mission of the church. That is our priceless heritage and estate.

At General Conference 2019, my fifth as a clergy delegate from the Arkansas Conference, I worked hard for the One Church Plan, hoping that we could find a way to keep most of us together. Like many others, I have come to the conclusion that our current situation is untenable, for conservatives, progressive, and moderates alike, and that we cannot sustain these levels of conflict and crisis. It is time to stop the fighting and to separate, either by outright division or by sweeping restructure, such as some version of the Connectional Conference Plan that will offer significant separation among the resulting groups.

The arguments in favor of separation or radical restructure have often been pragmatic and functional, emphasizing the current situation is not working. And the arguments against separation have often been more overtly theological, focusing on the theological unity of the church in Christ. I argue here that within our traditions of Methodism, the arguments for separation or radical restructure are deeply compelling and profoundly rooted in our own theology, especially our ecclesiology. Indeed, from its early days, Methodist ecclesiology has been much more clearly shaped by a vision for mission than unity.

Methodist ecclesiology is not an obvious place to turn in search of greater clarity; we are not known for a highly developed and fulsome theology of the church. In 1962, as talks were underway for a merger between the Methodist Church and the Evangelical United Brethren and as Methodists and EUB representatives joined with other Protestant denominations in the organization of the Consultation on Church Union (CoCU), Methodist scholars gathered at Oxford to discuss Methodism's doctrine of the church. It was not clear at the time that we even had one. When Albert Outler asked the group, "Do Methodists have a doctrine of the church?" his reply reflected the ambiguity with which we still live: "The answer 'yes' says too much; 'no' says too little. 'In a manner of speaking,' which is more nearly accurate than the other two, seems nevertheless equivocal."[1] In the intervening decades—longer than the lifespan of The United Methodist Church—scholars have continued to ask the same question and their replies still reflect Outler's ambivalence.

For all the disagreement, there is near unanimity that our United Methodist ecclesiology is, for good or ill, functional. We tend to make decisions about church, about structure, about our rules, based on what works, on what is good for our mission, for holiness of heart and life, holiness of individuals, communities, and even the world. Wesley's most often quoted line about ecclesiology comes from a letter written to John Smith who had accused him of setting aside the regular order of the church. Wesley wrote, "What is the end of all ecclesiastical order? Is it not to bring souls from the power of Satan to God, and to build them up in his fear and love? Order, then, is so far valuable as it answers these ends: and if it answers them not, it is nothing worth."[2] Like Wesley before us, we ask of any church structure or process, will it bring people to the power of God? Anyone who attended or watched General Conference 2019 would find it difficult to make the case that it brought people closer to the power of God and built them up in God's love.

Wesleyans have often been accused of subordinating theology to function when making decisions about church and polity, of setting aside theologically grounded decisions about church life in favor of

---

[1] Albert Outler, "Do Methodists Have a Doctrine of the Church," *The Doctrine of the Church,* Dow Kirkpatrick, ed. (Abingdon Press, 1964), 11.

[2] John Wesley, "Letter to John Smith," June 25, 1746, Letters II, vol. 26, *The Works of John Wesley,* Frank Baker, ed. (Abingdon Press, 1982), 206.

utilitarian calculations about what works, especially for our mission. More recently, Wesleyan scholars have countered with the insistence that giving priority to the function of the church in carrying out its mission is itself a theological claim; our theology of the church is mission centered. These arguments have taken different directions. Richard Heitzenrater, for example, has insisted that within Methodism the church is best understood theologically as a means of grace. For Heitzenrater, thinking of the church as a means of grace is a way to bring together the theological and functional, what the church is and what the church does. Methodism was organized from the beginning to be a means of God's grace, leading people toward greater love of God and neighbor, toward holiness of heart and life, toward forming and reforming not only each other but also larger communities, like churches and towns, even nations and continents.[33]

Doug Koskela makes a similar theological argument, insisting that United Methodist structure, polity, and processes are ultimately about discipline which is "the various commitments and practices by which a community of faith seeks to fulfill its calling ... the means by which Methodists hold each other accountable in their response to God's grace and their pursuit of holiness."[4] The point of our disciplines, our structures and practices, the ways we organize ourselves as a church, is to further our mission of holiness of life and heart.

By either theological model, church as means of grace toward holiness or church and polity as disciplines toward holiness, The United Methodist Church as a larger institutional body is not doing well. Our structure, which was set up to facilitate mission, is interfering with it. The point I am making is that we are in a mess not just because people are being difficult (which we are) or because we have experienced demographic changes (which we have) or because we are in a public relations disaster (which we are). No, it goes much deeper than that.

Our polity, structure, and institutions, set up to facilitate mission, are now interfering with our mission. They are no longer a means of grace but of sin, not of discipline but disorder and disunity.

---

[3] Richard Heitzenrater, "Wesleyan Ecclesiology: Methodism as a Means of Grace," in *Orthodox and Wesleyan Ecclesiology,* S.T. Kimbrough, ed. (St. Vladimir's Seminary Press, 2007), 119-128. See also Scott Jones, *United Methodist Doctrine: The Extreme Center* (Abingdon Press, 2002), 255-256 and Ted Campbell, "Methodist Ecclesiologies and Methodist Sacred Spaces" in *Orthodox and Wesleyan Ecclesiology,* S.T. Kimbrough, ed. (St. Vladimir's Seminary Press, 2007), 215-227.

[4] Douglas Koskela, "Discipline and Polity in *The Cambridge Companion to American Methodism,* Jason E. Vickers, ed. (Cambridge University Press, 2013), 156. See also Thomas Frank, *Polity, Practice and Mission of The United Methodist Church* (Abingdon, 2006).

It is bad for our souls, for our holiness. In this mess, we find ourselves at odds with our most deeply held, central beliefs about the church and our mission.

It is not the first time that our structure and polity have impeded mission. At the close of the 18th century, Bishops Coke and Asbury, in a robust defense of the offices of bishop and presiding elder, compared the Methodist church to a "vast machine." The role of the bishops is not to focus on the small details but "to preserve in order and in motion the wheels of the vast machine—to keep a constant and watchful eye upon the whole—and to think deeply for the general good." Russell Richey writes of Methodism using their image of a vast machine. Throughout its history, American Methodists have moved back and forth between glorying in their machinery and agonizing over it. Methodists have set up vast structures for the sake of their mission and gloried in the fruitfulness. Then, when the machinery began to hinder the mission, they agonized, denouncing the machinery, rebelling against it, taking it apart, and then proceeding to set up and glory in another structure set up for the sake of mission. The structure and machinery over which "one generation glories becoming the agonies of a later one."[5]

Dana Robert and Doug Tzan have identified a similar pattern in what they call the "Methodist mission paradigm." Methodists establish missions that bear fruit and a structure grows up around them to offer support. Over time, the structure no longer furthers but instead hinders the mission. Robert and Tzan write, "The history of Methodism, therefore, is a cycle of successful mission movements followed by institutionalization, followed by rebellions against institutionalization in the name of renewing the mission."[6]

It is fair to ask an obvious question, if we have been through this before, why not just move on through the cycle? Why is it so difficult to follow our usual Methodist pattern, getting beyond the agony of this structure and going on to the glory of a new one? It is different this time, because over the last century we have come to give theological priority to unity and connection over function and mission, and we have set up a structure that embodies that privileging of unity over mission.

Many today resist splitting The United Methodist Church for

---

[5] Russell Richey, "Methodism as Machine," in *Church, Identity, and Change: Theological and Denominational Structures in Unsettled Times*, David Roozen and James Nieman, eds. (Eerdmans Press, 2005), 533.

[6] Dana Robert and Douglas Tzan, "Traditions and Transitions in Mission Thought," *The Oxford Handbook of Methodist Studies*, William Abraham and James Kirby, eds. (Oxford University Press, 2009), 431.

theological reasons, a desire to avoid schism and to maintain the unity of the body of Christ. And in our laudable desire to avoid schism, we are carrying on a deep impulse of the last century of Methodism which sought to turn away from the earlier divisions of American Methodism and move toward greater unity. Russell Richey notes that in their first century, American Methodists were schism happy. They divided every decade. Schism, Richey writes, "might be termed American Methodism's ecclesial signature, or to change the image, its birthright."[7] The twentieth century rejected the pattern of division, and Methodists sought greater unity, bringing together the Methodist Churches North and South and the Methodist Protestant church in 1939 and the Methodists and the Evangelical United Brethren in 1968. By many measures, the last century of American Methodism was extraordinarily successful in avoiding of schism and embracing of unity. It brought together groups previously divided and staved off many renegade attempts to leave the denomination.

Elsewhere, Richey describes how among recent Methodists, connectionalism came to play a more central role in Methodist self-understanding, shaping the vision and mission. Perhaps because of the dissolution of community and connection in U.S. culture, connectionalism took on greater importance than in previous generations.[8] But this love of connection and unity was not the whole story.

Richey insists that if the twnetieth century Methodist story line was schism avoidant and unity friendly, the reality was more complicated. In the last century the fights have not driven the parties apart into several denominations, but have remained internal, fracturing the denomination from within. Richey writes, "schism continued but in a new mode." The arguments and power plays were internal, among caucus groups and regions of the church. "On the face of it then, the twentieth century may appear to have reversed the separatist spirit and put us together. On the structural plane, unification does indeed seem to have been our cause. . . In reality, division took different forms in the twentieth century."[9]

More critical for Methodist ecclesiology and life is the way these conflicts have shaped the mission of the church and the direction of

---

[7] Russell E. Richey, "Today's Untied Methodism: Living with/into/beyond Its Two Centuries of Regular Division" (The General Board of Higher Education and Ministry, 2017), 2.

[8] Russell Richey, "Connection and Connectionalism," *The Oxford Handbook of Methodist Studies,* William Abraham and James Kirby, eds. (Oxford University Press, 2009), 212-228. See also *Connectionalism: Ecclesiology, Mission, and Identity,* Russell Richey, Dennis Campbell, and William Lawrence eds. (Abingdon Press, 1997).

[9] Richey, "Today's Untied Methodism," pp. 1 and 6.

its gaze. In the earlier days of American Methodism when divisions were common, the focus of the churches, albeit now divided, was directed outward. Indeed the divisions fueled a competitive spirit as the new denominations vied with one another for faithfulness and members. The original denomination may have fractured, but the resulting smaller denominations grew rapidly. By contrast, the current ongoing state of internal denominational schism has left The United Methodist Church inward focused, undermining its mission, the very thing that gives it meaning and purpose.

It is not a stretch to call our internal division and contention by the word schism. Indeed, when an elderly John Wesley examined biblical texts on schism, he found that the clear biblical meaning was not "a separation *from* any Church . . . but a separation *in* a Church." At eighty-two, he had witnessed not only great holiness and even perfection among Christians but also great perfidy and vileness. Schism, Wesley insisted, is "alienation of affection" and "division of heart" among members of the same church. And this division of heart tears a wide path of destruction. It increases "unkind tempers, both in ourselves and others" and sets in motion harsh and unfair judgments against each other, anger, resentment, and hatred, "creating a present hell...as a prelude to hell eternal." And this bitterness of heart then shows itself in bitter words and ultimately in sinful action. Out of this trail of bitter hearts, words and actions, "thousands of souls" are driven from faith and peace and toward misery and separation from God, "and finally drowned in everlasting perdition." Wesley warned his early Methodists, "He whose heart is full of prejudice, anger, suspicion, or any unkind temper, will surely open his mouth in a manner corresponding with the disposition of his mind. And hence will arise, if not lying and slandering, (which yet will hardly be avoided,) bitter words, talebearing, backbiting, and evil-speaking of every kind." [10] What a fitting description of our current United Methodist conflicts and our 2019 General Conference!

Just a few years before, Wesley had written a sermon "Of Evil Angels" where he described the methods Satan and his minions use to attack human beings and Christ's church. Satan's primary strategy is to destroy human love for one other, and he and his evil angels are always watching for any opportunity, even and especially among the faithful. Just as "every good thought, or word, or action" is done in cooperation with God and is a fruit of the Holy Spirit, so "every evil thought, or word, or work" is in cooperation with and a "fruit of the evil spirit." Satan uses "every possible means to prevent

---

[10] John Wesley, "On Schism," *Sermons III: 71–114,vol. 3, The Works of John Wesley* (Abingdon Press, 1986), §§ I.1; I.7; and I.12-14.

or destroy [love of neighbor]; to excite either private or public suspicions, animosities, resentment, quarrels; to destroy the peace of families or of nations; and to banish unity and concord from the earth. And this, indeed, is the triumph of his art; to embitter the poor, miserable children of men against each other, and at length urge them to do his own work, to plunge one another into the pit of destruction."[11] Here we have another apt description of General Conference and our present United Methodist conflicts! I am not saying that we can blame Satan for our current conflicts; there is plenty of blame to go around! Plain old human sin and frailty can account for most it, but the level of pain and distrust was so high at General Conference 2019, that it is difficult not to wonder about evil forces beyond human understanding.

For all his suspicion of evil angels as the underlying cause of human conflict and his opposition to schism, whether as internal rancor or external separation, Wesley did acknowledge that there were occasions when actual division was appropriate. When the church had reached a point when a Christian "could not continue therein with a clear conscience," separation was justified.[12] We have a reached a point when many of our members, indeed our leaders, are in crises of conscience. Many conservatives face a struggle of conscience to support a church that would allow gay and lesbian people to be married, ordained, and serve as bishops. Many progressives and now moderates face a struggle of conscience to support a church that not only disallows those things but also imposes unprecedently harsh penalties on those whose conscience demands disobedience on these matters. One of many oddities of our current crisis is that we are rent apart by conscience, by good people whose consciences are leading them in different directions.

The antagonism and rancor that Wesley describes and that has bedeviled the history not only of Methodism but of the whole Christian church has its own peculiar cast in The United Methodist Church today. Our current debates in The United Methodist Church are more fraught and more fractured, because many of its leaders are a part of the United States context which has seen a rapid polarization of its people (left and right); an increase in hate and hate speech; and a deterioration of civility. The brutal fights of The United Methodist Church today are shaped in part by the peculiar culture wars of the United States.

---

[11] John Wesley, "Of Evil Angels," *Sermons III: 71–114, vol. 3, The Works of John Wesley* (Abingdon Press, 1986), §§ II.9 and II.5.

[12] Wesley, "On Schism," § I.17.

So here we are. We have over the last century given theological priority to unity over mission. We have set up a structure that embodies that desire for unity and connection by making separation harder. Yet the effect has not been to leave us more unified but only to keep the divisions growing more contentious within, internalizing schism. All of that has served to keep our attention focused inward and to weaken our sacred estate—our mission.

Whatever the cause or medley of causes, our current situation is ugly. Since the division and levels of distrust are so high, it is extremely difficult to find even the minimal amount of cooperation needed to get voices and votes together to find any way out of the ugliness. It is easy to say we should find a path to separation or restructure; it is much harder to come up with proposals that will actually get through General Conference. What an irony that we must foster greater unity and cooperation to find a path to separation.

If we are not able to find a path to separation or restructure then, for the love of God and our mission, we must be ready to cut each other and our ministries lose. We need to give churches and annual conference the freedom to reorganize themselves, taking their resources with them. We must give our institutions the right to affiliate with the church in new ways, for example, in a broader pan-Methodist affiliation, or even to disaffiliate if they choose, so that our universities, hospitals, and other bodies are not diminished by church discord.

But I still have hope and confidence that we can find a path to organized separation or restructure, for two simple Wesleyan reasons. First, though you could not have proved it by our behavior at the 2019 General Conference, we are a disciplined people familiar with the spiritual practices that will foster the forgiveness, humility, love, and peace without which we will never reach agreement.

Second, I believe that we will stop short of fighting to the death, because we hold so dear our family estate—our mission. With the Igbo people, we know that "When brothers and sisters fight to the death, a stranger inherits the father's estate."

**Rebekah Miles** is Professor of Ethics and Practical Theology at Perkins School of Theology at Southern Methodist University. An ordained elder in the Arkansas Conference, Miles has been clergy delegate to five General Conferences. She writes in the areas of Wesleyan ethics, Christian realism, and practical theology. Miles is the author, co-author or editor of six books, including *When the One You Love is Gone* (Nashville: Abingdon Press, 2012); *Georgia Harkness: The Remaking of a Liberal Theo-logian, Collected Essays from 1929-1942* (Louisville: Westminster John Knox, 2010); *The Bonds of Freedom: Feminist Theology and Christian Realism* (Oxford University Press, 2001); *The Pastor as Moral Guide* (Fortress Press, 1999); and *Wesley and the Quadrilateral: Renewing the Conversation* (Abingdon Press, 1997). Miles speaks here for herself and not as a representative of Southern Methodist University.

# CHAPTER NINETEEN
# Chris Ritter
## 2020 Visions

You may have never heard of a Snellen chart, but you almost certainly have seen one. Most of us at some point have stood in the hallway of a medical office, one eye covered, to read the letters under the large capital "E." If visual acuity is average, a person is said to have 20/20 vision. This means a patient can see clearly from twenty feet what most people can see at that same distance. The Snellen chart is so common that 20/20 has become a synonym for clarity.

2020 does not mean clarity for United Methodists. Now that St. Louis has revealed the depths of our theological divisions, our denomination seems to be on a path toward an undetermined structural reordering. We know there will be a UM General Conference in 2020. Who will attend? What will delegates come to Minneapolis to do? Unlike the months prior to GC2019, there is no single group charged with defining and developing possible options for the future. The Council of Bishops, temporarily invited into the legislative process, spent that influence on a plan that failed acceptance. Divided among themselves as the rest of the church, the council is now effectively sidelined. The Connectional Table has offered to insert itself into the post-GC2019 conversation, but their past advocacy for liberalizing proposals disqualifies them as a neutral broker.[1] Private, sober, *ad hoc* conversations and caucusing are underway.[2] But to what end?

---

[1] "For the Sake of the Church - A Statement in the Aftermath of the Special Session," The Connectional Table, accessed April 3, 2019, http://s3.amazonaws.com/Website_Properties/news-media/press-center/documents/Statement_Translations.pdf .

See also their earlier advocacy for a proto-One Church Plan here:
Hahn, Heather, "Church body seeks greater openness on human sexuality," May 18, 2015, UMNews.org, https://www.umnews.org/en/news/church-body-seeks-greater-openness-on-human-sexuality.

[2] Hodges, Sam, "Denomination's future under discussion — quietly," April 1, 2019, UMNews.org, https://www.umnews.org/en/news/denominations-future-under-discussion-quietly.

The Western Jurisdiction and other thoroughly progressive conferences have not yet determined a course of action beyond organized defiance to the UM disciplines around sexuality. Adam Hamilton has promised a May 2019 meeting of five hundred leaders and a wider forum in the fall during his annual Leadership Institute.[3] He is part of a Progressive-Centrist conversation group that held its first meeting in Dallas in March. Hamilton speaks of a "New Methodism," but there is no word yet on what shape he hopes that might take.[4] Bishop Haupert-Johnson, leader of the largest U.S. annual conference, was quoted in *The Washington Times* as favoring a split.[5] The Wesley Covenant Association has decided to stay for now, but has indicated that their patience with defiance to our United Methodist covenants is limited and that they hope for a quick and final resolution.

My own part in this has been as a solution-seeker and commentator. A self-avowed, practicing traditionalist, I was perhaps the most recognizable delegate supporting the Connectional Conference Plan at GC2019. I now believe that door to be firmly shut. Conferring with African delegates convinced me they could never support such a diversification of ethical teachings under the umbrella of the UMC. African United Methodists do not have the urgency and anxiety around this issue that we in the West do. Like the One Church Plan, they view the CCP as the UMC lending its good name to the practice of homosexuality. Lack of African support is fatal to the ratification process needed by any structural plans capable of keeping all the current players in the same denomination. While a grand structural solution might have worked with strong episcopal support prior to 2019, the CCP is now dead.

Deciding to divorce is painful. Getting divorced is complicated. Complexity is infinitely multiplied in our intertwined global denomination with multiple power centers. Amidst our significant uncertainties, I see four possible paths for General Conference 2020. Here is that list of "2020 Visions" in no particular order.

[3] Hamilton, Adam, "An Update on the Denomination," March 29, 2019, Cor.org, https://cor.org/west/blog/an-update-on-the-denomination.

[4] Hamilton, Adam, "A New United Methodism?" March 8, 2019, AdamHamilton.com, https://www.adamhamilton.com/blog/a-new-united-methodism#.XJ4tty2ZNN0.

[5] Zauzmer, Julie, "U.S. Methodist leaders lay plans to resist vote against same-sex marriage," March 29, 2019, WashingtonPost.com, https://www.washingtonpost.com/religion/2019/03/29/us-methodist-leaders-lay-plans-resist-anti-gay-marriage-vote/.

## Vision One: Restage the Battle of 2019

General Conference 2019 was billed as a high-profile, special-ly-called, and prayer-soaked global meeting to bring final resolution to the UMC's disagreements over human sexuality. We now have a decision, complete with winners and losers. What we don't have is a settlement. The winners do not feel like winners. The losers do not accept the outcome. Instead of pouring water on our house fire, we are adding gasoline.

The fact that another General Conference is happening just next year has created an interesting wrinkle. Some who believe GC2019 got it wrong hold onto hope that GC2020 will get it right. These hopes might be buoyed by an April 2019 Judicial Council decision that sets aside as unconstitutional the legislation enacted as part of the Traditional Plan. An argument could be made by progressives that nothing legal was decided and that we need a do-over.

This vision is articulated by retired Bishop Mike Coyner. In an editorial published by United Methodist New Service, Coyner argues that the results of GC2019 were rather predictable given it involved the same delegates as 2016.[6] More people open to change may be elected to GC2020. Good ideas like the One Church Plan, he posits, take time to gain acceptance. We have seen the movement to change church policies swell dramatically in the U.S. and it is possible this trend could overtake the growing number of Central Conference delegates. The One Church Plan almost won in 2019 and has another opportunity in 2020 now that we know the aftermath of its rejection.

Bishop Coyner's analysis omits some important facts. While electing more progressives is clearly a strategy in play, leaders on both sides have done the math and have concluded at the battle for control of General Conference is over.[7] If the One Church Plan was not accepted on the silver platter on which it was served, it is doubt-ful it could ever pass otherwise. GC2019 was a last-ditch, hail-Mary, high-profile effort to change UMC teachings on human sexuality. Even if progressives could somehow eke out an upset, this would trigger an

---

[6] Coyner, Bishop Michael J., "Opinion: 'What's next for our United Methodist Church?'" March 13, 2019, https://www.umnews.org/en/news/opinion-whats-next-for-our-unit-ed-methodist-church.

[7] Lambrecht, Thomas, "Doing General Conference Math," March 25, 2019, Good News-mag.org, https://goodnewsmag.org/2019/03/doing-general-conference-math/. See also Holland, Rev. Dr. Mark R., "5 Reasons to consider a U.S. Church," April 3, 2019, https://mainstreamumc.com/blog/5-reasons-to-consider-a-u-s-church/.

exit of U.S. Traditionalists that would only speed Central Conference numerical dominance. *The Washington Post* characterizes Bishop Sue Haupert-Johnson as saying that the U.S. church will "increasingly be under the thumb of African voters" unless a split occurs.[8]

It is exactly because of the African church that some U.S. Evangelicals believe they must dig the trenches for a longer fight. Joe Kilpatrick, a long-time lay delegate in the North Georgia Conference, sent a message to leaders in Traditionalist renewal movements encouraging them not to rush for compromise, but to push for passage of the rest of the Traditional Plan.[9] He is speaking of a measure that would encourage annual conferences unwilling to support the Book of Discipline to leave. This measure was shuffled off to a committee at GC2019 and not included in the legislation ultimately approved. It would have required a vote in each annual conference and provided a mechanism for those unwilling to follow the UM Discipline to leave with their assets.

Kilpatrick reminds U.S. Traditionalists that African delegates, the key votes at GC2019, want as much unity as possible along with the respected United Methodist name and logo. They also could use United Methodist money. He mentions $87 million in unrestricted liquid reserves that are part of $402 million in general church assets. He argues:

> Let's remember the great needs in Africa; seminaries using out-houses, students cooking their meals on fires, student families growing their corn and veggies, pastors riding on bicycles to serve communion in a distant village with inadequate public transportation, UMC elementary and secondary schools with no printed materials, broken sewing machines and outdated computers in vocational training classes; UM hospitals with broken X-rays, broken lighting in operating rooms, broken bathrooms in the wards, and the list goes on. [10]

In other words: Amidst all the rainbows, Traditionalists should not lose sight of the pots of gold.

Kilpatrick believes that the legislative power of General Conference can eventually overcome the resistance to be encountered from bishops elected for life and an entrenched bureaucracy. Passing more

---

[8] Zauzmer, "U.S. Methodist leaders lay plans to resist vote against same-sex marriage."

[9] Kilpatrick, Joe, "A Friend of the UMC in Africa Asks U.S. Traditionalists to Not Give Up on Renewal and Reform," PeopleNeedJesus.files.wordpress.com, https://people-needjesus.files.wordpress.com/2019/03/joe-kilpatrick-dont-give-up-on-umc-reform.pdf.

[10] Kilpatrick, "A Friend of the UMC in Africa Asks U.S. Traditionalists to Not Give Up on Renewal and Reform."

episcopal accountability measures and increasing the number of African bishops will eventually bring the significant reform the church needs.[11]

As demonstrated here, at least some combatants on both sides are ready to re-engage next year. Can the UMC brand sustain another battle like the one that raged in St. Louis? Or would restaging the battle of 2019 follow the Vietnam era logic of destroying the village in order to save it? These questions bring us to a second option.

## Vision Two: More than One General Conference

In the 1980's movie *War Games*, a computer simulation plays out all the possible scenarios for global thermonuclear war. Just prior to launching its missiles, the computer grasps the concept of mutual assured destruction and comments that nuclear war is a "strange game" in that "the only winning move is not to play." A "nice game of chess" is suggested instead.

The prospects of a protracted denominational war of attrition are wearisome. Many progressives have come to view General Conference as a game that cannot be won. Whatever else the One Church Plan was, it was not a stable solution for United Methodism. It was only acceptable to Progressives as a transitional state to full inclusion. To go back to General Conference 2020 and argue otherwise would betray some important core principles of justice. Given what progressives want from GC2020 is something they know they cannot get, one solution is simply to not show up. Deciding not to play the old game allows space to organize something new.

The prospects of starting from scratch are attractive. We serve a post-denominational culture in which established "brand name" versions of faith have little strategic advantage. After fifty years at sea, our UMC ship has a lot of barnacles on the hull. Efforts to reform our bureaucracy have been frustrated by a rigid institutionalism that protects the status quo. The 2019 human sexuality vote is not the only source of frustration for progressives. The UMC is becoming more pro-life in its stance on abortion. Participation in the Religious Coalition for Reproductive Choice was banned in 2016. A long-standing resolution supporting the Roe v. Wade decision was allowed to expire that same year. In spite of the fact that our general agencies are strongholds of institutionalized progressivism, action on those convictions is frustrated by our legislative branch.

---

[11] Abraham, William J., "Abraham: Mountains are there to be climbed," March 17, 2019, PeopleNeedJesus.net, https://peopleneedjesus.net/2019/03/17/abraham-mountains-are-there-to-be-climbed-the-next-united-methodism/.

Under Vision Two, progressive United Methodists would hold their own organizing event for a fresh expression of Methodism. Whole annual conferences would join this movement along with individual congregations across the U.S. and Western Europe.

There is also the possibility of a Centrist expression of Methodism developing independent of GC2020 for those who might want to pursue the vision distinct from the program of full inclusion. Adam Hamilton, Tom Berlin, and others have focused on local church effectiveness and are willing to accept diversity of practice with regards to inclusion. They look circumspectly at the entrenched obsolescence of our denominational structures. They may view the United Methodist "brand" as damaged beyond repair due to the fallout from GC2019 and seek to form a moderate Methodism with a renewed focus on the American ideological mainstream.

Could 2020 be the year of three separate general conferences? This is unlikely. The strongest bastions of progressivism have long skirted UM rules without consequence and are more than willing to hang on and have voice in the significant unresolved legal and structural issues to be decided. It is likely that all parties will show up to GC2020, if only to make sure they get a fair cut of the UM estate.

One way to end the fighting is for one side to not show up. Another is to come together to make peace.

## Vision Three: A Constitutional Convention

A third option for GC2020 is to replace our current constitution (and, therefore, our denomination) with something totally new. We could treat our meeting in Minneapolis like something of a constitutional convention. This would mean tabling all human sexuality petitions (and other unfruitful business) to focus on creating the structural space that might allow us to continue together. What if The United Methodist Church became, instead, a United Methodist communion of churches?

A communion is a family of autonomous denominations and/or regional churches. One example would be the Orthodox churches which have full communion with each other among their independently headed churches. An example closer to Methodism is the Anglican Communion.

Unity in Anglicanism is expressed in several ways, but there is nothing like a General Conference coming together to edit a central *Book of Discipline*. The body that comes closest is the seventy-member Anglican Consultative Council meeting every three years. It elects its own officers and chooses several members to serve in

160

something like our General Council on Finance and Administration. The bishops of the communion gather only once each decade. There is also a Secretary General who is empowered to hire whatever staff the communion requires for its operations. A structure of this limited scope is sufficient because it is not directly governing the member churches, only overseeing the expressions of Anglicanism they all share.

Communions are not without conflict. The Episcopal Church, for instance, was suspended from participation in 2016. The issue was... wait for it...the topic of human sexuality. But these disagreements do little to disrupt the operation of each member church. Communions operate as a cooperative, voluntary fellowship of denominations.

*"An entirely new constitution would need to be drafted, approved and ratified."*

A United Methodist Communion would need to be spacious, more spacious I expect, than the Anglican Communion. It would primarily serve as a way to share common assets and maintain a modicum of coordination as an alternative to total separation.

Getting to such a markedly different structure is an onerous task. An entirely new constitution would need to be drafted, approved and ratified. Then, there is the process of moving conferences and congregations into new denominations. The mechanism for this will need to be detailed enough to address the complexities of our current crisis. We can draw much wisdom from the Connectional Conference Plan (CCP) which was framed for a similar purpose. The CCP called for each jurisdiction and central conference to choose a new branch to join (or become its own). Those annual conferences that disagreed could vote to join a different branch. Local churches in disharmony with their annual conference could also opt into a different branch. This keeps divisive local voting, unavoidable though it is, to a minimum.

Some days of General Conference 2020 could be dedicated to the preliminary formation of the member churches of a UM communion. Realistically, I think we would need one church comprised of committed progressive conferences, one church for American centrists, and a Global Methodism comprised of U.S. Evangelicals, Filipinos, Eastern Europeans, and Africans. It is possible that some central conferences may prefer to be their own church within the communion. This, again, mirrors options offered by the CCP.

When it comes to branding the various churches in a United Methodist Communion, I would think that the United Methodist name should not be used by any member church without the addition of specifying language. No group may call themselves "The United Methodist Church." They could, however, adopt names like "Progressive Methodist Church," "United Methodist Church of the Philippines," or "Global Methodist Church." No church may use the standard cross and flame as its primary identity, but each may develop a distinct version of the cross and flame should they so choose.

If the UMC became the United Methodist Communion, perhaps other Methodist churches around the world might want to participate, too. [12] The communion may become a richer expression of the unity we now enjoy among the eighty denominations of the World Methodist Council. Perhaps the African Methodist Episcopal Church, Christian Methodist Episcopal Church, and AME, Zion churches might want to open renewed dialog with us. (The role of bishops has always been a sticking point in unification talks and this would no longer be an issue in a broad UM Communion.) It would take years for these unifying ideas to develop. However, building something new together might take the sting out of the death of the denomination.

## Vision Four: Formal Division

If debating human sexuality again is fruitless, and if ad hoc separation is impractical, and if staying in the same institution is too complicated, that leaves us with one other option: formal division. Under this scenario, General Conference 2020 would come together to decide on terms of divorce. Many, including a number of United Methodist academics from across the theological spectrum,[13] have concluded this is the point at which we have regrettably arrived. However, it is not as easy as simply deciding to separate.

---

[12] The language of "association" has also been suggested. The UMC would become an association of denominations with a group of shared agencies.

[13] An example for the theological center would be Kent Millard, President of United Theological Seminary. His comments can be read at:
Millard, Kent, "Reflections on UMC General Conference," March 1, 2019, https://united.edu/president-millard-umc-general-conference/.

From the theological left, we have statements from Perkins' O Wesley Allen, Jr.:
Allen, O. Wesley, Jr., "Humpty Dumpty Can't Be Put Back Together Again: Why The United Methodist Church Must Split," March 28, 2019, http://hackingchristianity.net/2019/03/guest-post-why-the-united-methodist-church-must-split.html.

and Claremont School of Theology's Jack Jackson:
Jackson, Jack, "A Hopeful Way Forward for Progressive United Methodists," March 25, 2019, https://um-insight.net/perspectives/a-hopeful-way-forward-for-progressive-united-methodists/.

On the traditional side we have Asbury Theological Seminary's Bill Arnold:
Arnold, Bill T., "General Conference 2020: Déjà vu All Over Again?" https://peopleneedjesus.net/2019/03/19/general-conference-2020-deja-vu-all-over-again/.

The UMC constitution stands in the way. It will need to be altered or otherwise navigated if conflicts are to end.

One model for division is dissolution.[14] An often-overlooked fact is that the UMC does not technically exist, at least not as a legal entity. It is more of an idea. Our denomination is comprised of separately incorporated general agencies, annual conferences, congregations, and other bodies that are tied to one another by covenants and property deeds. If you take the plastic connector off a six-pack of Dr. Pepper, the individual cans are free to roll around where they will. If The United Methodist Church dissolved, each piece would be set free to decide how and whether to be in relationship with the others.

Dissolution is an attractive form of division in that it avoids the win/lose scenario of one group showing another group the door. A significant challenge is that it requires a constitutional amendment to allow suspension of our constitution. Amendments must be passed by a super majority and ratified around the world. African bishops prior to GC2019 expressed their opposition to dissolving the UMC.[15] A legally-sanctioned dissolution plan would face uncertain prospects of approval and would take years to implement.

Another model is a formal plan of division approved at GC2020. Rather than dissolve, the UMC, through General Conference, would decide how it will divide into two or more successor bodies. Like dissolution, a formal plan of division would avoid a winner-take-all approach to our battle over human sexuality. Still, division also has constitutional ramifications and must meet the high bar of super-majority passage and ratification.

Is there a way to divide the denomination without altering our constitution? Yes. The Modified Traditional Plan contained an extended paragraph that provides annual conferences a mechanism to leave with their properties intact.[16] The mechanism for annual

---

[14] Keith Boyette, president of the Wesleyan Covenant Association, submitted legislation that would accomplish dissolution to GC2019. It was ruled out of harmony with the call of General Conference and not considered.

[15] Yambasu, Bishop John K., "Africa College of Bishops Learning Retreat Freetown, Sierra Leone Statement," accessed April 4, 2019, http://s3.amazonaws.com/Website_Properties/news-media/press-center/documents/Africa_College_of_Bishops_Learning_Retreat_2018_statement.pdf.

[16] See Petition 90079 in General Conference 2019's Advance Daily Christian Advocate, page 212 at: "2019 Special Session of The General Conference The United Methodist Church," Commission on the General Conference, accessed April 4, 2019, http://cdn-files.umc.org/Website_Properties/general-conference/2019/documents/general-conference-2019-adca-english.pdf.

conference exit has already been ruled constitutional by our Judicial Council.[17] The petition, however, was deemed to have implications in the Central Conferences and was referred to a standing committee where it died. There was no time at GC2019 to bring this back as a minority report for passage. Something like it, however, could be approved by a simple majority at General Conference 2020.

Here is how the mechanism, if passed, would work. Following General Conference, each annual conference would take a vote on whether it can uphold the *Book of Discipline* as written. Those that cannot are invited into a process whereby they can leave the denomination by a simple majority vote. When they do so, their jurisdictional or central conference convenes to remap the territory they are vacating on the UMC map. Individual churches in the departing conference have a space of time in which they can vote to stay in the UMC. These churches go into a conference assigned by their jurisdiction to receive them. Those conferences and congregations that leave would hold their own organizing event for a new denomination, perhaps cloning some of the UMC *Discipline* for the sake of continuity.

A sticking point in any sort of future re-sorting of United Methodists is our Judicial Council's unexpected interpretation of constitutional ¶41. This obscure provision was written to govern the process whereby a local church might leave a missionary conference for a standard conference, and vice versa. In recent decisions, however, the Judicial Council applied the processes in ¶41 to any UMC congregation moving to another conference or similar body.[18] It requires a two-third vote by the charge conference, the congregation, the conference being exited, and the conference receiving them. This has created a situation where it is potentially much easier for an entire conference to leave the UMC than for a single congregation to do so. Whatever else we do in 2020, ¶41 should be repealed or replaced so that we can achieve the fluidity we need for workable congregational transfers.

Using a feature of the Traditional Plan as a mechanism for separation may partially retain the win/lose dynamic we hope to avoid. Although the Plan spells out that departing conferences may utilize services from any of the UMC general agencies, those conferences do

---

[17] "Judicial Council of The United Methodist Church Decision No. 1366," Judicial Council, accessed April 4, 2019, http://cdnfiles.umc.org/Website_Properties/JCD_1366_(Docket_No._1018-12).pdf.

[18] This interpretation was first given in Judicial Council Decision 1366 found at: "Judicial Council of The United Methodist Church Decision No. 1366," http://cdnfiles.umc.org/Website_Properties/JCD_1366_(Docket_No._1018-12).pdf.

not share in the governance of those agencies. If The United Methodist Church stays in place, those exiting may feel like exiles.

I believe there are ways to mitigate the win/lose dynamic. One option is to spin off the general agencies of the UMC as autonomous non-profits that provide services to whatever judicatory might require them.[19] Instead of our general agencies being run by boards populated by the jurisdictional conferences, they would operate under boards perpetuated by their own processes. Annual conferences, whether inside or outside the UMC, could contract with these agencies for services related to pensions, discipleship, ordained ministry, etc. The general agencies would have to survive in the free market instead of receiving funding from a denominational umbilical cord. Change will come to our general agencies regardless. A draconian twenty-three percent budget cut in agency funding has already been recommended to GC2020 due to denominational decline.[20]

> *"I say these things not as a skeptic or to deny scriptural authority, but as one who consistently fails to be faithful."*

Autonomous general agencies give United Methodists less to fight over or reform. Another means of making the separation mechanism in the Traditional Plan more palatable to those leaving the UMC would be an agreement to retire the United Methodist name, at least in the United States. The structure of the UMC would continue to exist, but it would do business by another name in America as a way of acknowledging the significant split.

## Conclusion

The shroud of unknowing that covers the future of our denomination will undoubted lift over the coming months. These four visions for 2020 are by no means exhaustive, but they represent a range of probable options for what may be the final General Conference of United Methodism as it has been known. May God smile on

---

[19] Wespath (formerly the General Board of Pensions and Health Benefits of The United Methodist Church) has paved the way by rebranding and positioning itself to offer services to any judicatory needing benefits support.

[20] Hahn, Heather, "Deciding what budget cuts mean for ministry," January 14, 2019, UMNews.org, https://www.umnews.org/en/news/deciding-what-budget-cuts-mean-for-ministry.

conversations happening behind the scenes and across the aisles that are aimed at staving off another incendiary gathering like we experienced in St. Louis. It will take God's grace to get us all through a contentious season of annual conference sessions to arrive in Minneapolis with a spirit of collaboration. One helpful tool in the meantime is a sense of history. The Christian story, especially Protestant history, is replete with schisms, reformations, and reunifications. In 2020, we will simply turn a page to the next chapter.

**Dr. Chris Ritter** is an ordained elder in the Illinois Great River Conference of The United Methodist Church which he represented as a General Conference delegate in 2016 and 2019. He serves as the Directing Pastor of Geneseo First UMC which has twice been recognized for high numbers of professions of faith during his tenure. He is the author of Seven Things John Wesley Expected Us to Do for Kids (Abingdon Press, 2016) and has contributed articles and chapters for publication on the topic of United Methodism's future. He holds a Master of Divinity degree from Candler School of Theology (Emory University, Atlanta) and a Doctor of Ministry in Evangelism from Perkins School of Theology (Southern Methodist University, Dallas). He and his wife of thirty years, Becky, have four young adult children. You can follow his blog at peopleneedjesus.net.

# CHAPTER TWENTY
# Don E. Saliers

Recovery, Wisdom, and Fidelity:
The Present Struggle

Emergency responders recognize degrees of trauma when they come to the aid of victims, and they can attest that victims of warfare incur deep traumas. Presently, The United Methodist Church is reeling from a social body trauma, and even though Christian churches have experienced warfare and wounding over millennia, we are not well-instructed or experienced in the facilitation of healing.

At this point, there is no easy healing (reconciliation) or recovery in our present impasse. Many have tried to explain our wounds. To some, the fault belongs to those who oppose "scriptural fidelity" and violate the laws of the church. We are seemingly caught in accusations and blame on all sides. The history of hardening divisions among United Methodists is part of the back story I leave to others to recite.

As in many cases of trauma, a way toward healing involves a collective remembering, wherever possible. Trauma can make the task of remembering difficult, as it can distort or prevent memory, but the assessment must be fully honest and self-critical.

In my judgment, we need both a "call to remembrance" and an affirmation of the eschatological basis of the Body of Christ. When has Methodist faith and life been "at its best" despite disagreements? There can be no nostalgia for a romanticized past. This process requires a deeper anamnesis, like the "remembering" in our prayers of Great Thanksgiving, in baptism, and the Lord's Supper. This very form of memory is a remembering the future by proclaiming what has been promised by God in Christ to both the church and the world.

Alfred Loisy (an ex-communicated French priest, 1857-1940) once quipped, "Jesus promised us the Kingdom, and we got the church instead." Some are tempted to say "... but we got the church instead."

We are struggling with that fundamental tension. How do we envision the relationship between the church, the world, and the reign of God? How is the church to faithfully order its life in the present age? What is a realistic and honest remembering of what Methodism is at its best?

I begin with our evangelical/catholic combination of faithful, theologically informed preaching, teaching, and sacramental life and practice infused with active personal and social holiness oriented to the Kingdom of God. This is the legacy of Wesley's "knowledge and vital piety." At our best, we have been able to teach and live both holiness of life and profound service and inclusion in the very process of offering a prophetic critique of the powers of the world.

Admittedly, this is an ideal picture. Yet, this is the Methodism I recall when the church has been most alive to its mission and reason for being. It still is. I have seen and heard this in many local congregations, large and small, urban and rural. I see it in the common energies devoted to agencies such as UMCOR and to faithful medical, educational, and social mission work in the United States and abroad. That is the Methodism (indeed, the whole Body of Christ) most of us still long for. That is the Methodist movement alive and well underneath all the fragmentation and struggles with cultural captivities of all kinds, including slavery in an earlier time.

What kind of "scriptural fidelity" and wise polity does this call for? Exclusion from leadership and the blessing of same-sex relationships is the issue, at least at the surface. Should such exclusion be made solely on the basis of traditional scriptural assumptions about gender and sexuality?

The exclusion of LGBTQIA+ persons from pastoral roles and consecrated marriages is a difficult matter. For some, especially our brothers and sisters in Africa and elsewhere, homosexuality is both legally prosecuted and culturally shunned. Any acceptance would place members of those churches in jeopardy. For others, both in Africa and the United States, homosexuality is thought to be against biblical teaching and, for some, a sickness or even a human "abomination."

So, what is the basis of exclusion? How does "scriptural fidelity" bear upon our decisions? What if we were to exclude from leadership those who fail to live up to the Sermon on the Mount or Matthew 25? The moral and spiritual failings of most of us would be fiercely evident. Who can live up to the radical demand of "when have you seen me hungry, or naked, or in prison and have cared for me?" Have we tended to the "orphans and the widows?" What about divorced persons? Jesus' teachings seem clear. Who among us is consistently a "peacemaker?" Who among us has attained "purity of heart?"

It is so difficult to avoid injuring others in our anger, our gossip, and our selfishness. When the Lord asks, as in the old gospel hymn, "Are Ye Able" to follow me all the way into the Kingdom, can we answer without irony or deception, "Lord, we are able, to the death we follow Thee?"

I say these things not as a skeptic or to deny scriptural authority, but as one who consistently fails to be faithful. How many times have I not lived up to my baptismal vows or the grace received in the Lord's Supper? Thank God there is more than human regret and remorse. There is mercy, and it is not exclusionary.

> *"I say these things not as a skeptic or to deny scriptural authority, but as one who consistently fails to be faithful."*

At the heart of biblical faith and Christian life is utter dependency on the mercy of Christ. There is no scriptural basis for exclusion when one fails to attain holiness. However, there is the exclusion of fear and judgment. We must begin by acknowledging unworthiness and then receive the grace that affirms the integrity of being created in the image of God. God does not see as we see, but "looks upon the heart." Thus, Jesus includes repentance in the prayer he gives the church.

Beyond disputes about scriptural interpretation, the fact is that our current polity is unworkable. The juridical/political model of governance we practice shows crucial limitations. At present, there is no forum for theological decision-making outside the annual, jurisdictional, and General conferences. We speak of scriptural authority, the "tradition," faithful experience, and uses of reason. However, in our adapted parliamentary procedures, we fail to utilize the Quadrilateral itself.

We need to know and respect one another before declaring winners and losers. There are many faithful Methodists who read Scripture much more conservatively than I do. Yet, their lives are exemplary and their passion for healing, faithful service, and care for others is true witness. Doctrinal disputes over theological anthropology are, in this sense, secondary, though not unimportant. When doctrinal purity becomes ideology, conservative or liberal, we can soon neglect the living relationship between members of the Body of Christ and our deeper origins in God's promises.

We cannot heal the present trauma by perpetuating the cultural "winner/loser mentality" to which we are now subject. Furthermore, as long as we continue to call out one another as enemies, we cannot abide. There are real and substantial differences among us. Four major contested areas of thought and practice that remain to separate us are as follows:

1. Our differing notions of "biblical fidelity" and how best to read scripture

2. How to define and live with "denominational law"

3. How we understand "faithful sexual expression of love"

4. How we understand "holiness" in light of the deeper spiritual sense of the word.

I can imagine us coming to certain intellectual understandings in each of these areas, and yet still being unable to embrace fellow Christians with whom we differ. Such embrace cannot emerge until we seek relationships between the "Kingdom of God" and the actual life and work of The United Methodist Church in our present world. This cannot be addressed by political cliques and attempts to deride and accuse one another.

Getting to know one another and participating in ministry together is crucial. When we blame one another with suspicion and find no way forward because our decision-making is structured to ignore powerful cultural differences, it is hard to come to any agreement about what the promised Kingdom asks of its churches today. Unhappy and non-Wesleyan schism is inevitable because of our weaknesses, not our strengths.

I cannot claim to speak for God, but I do have my own family and my own pastoral experiences with lesbian and gay struggles. I have learned so much from them about grace and wisdom. Yet, further critical, collaborative reflection may still lead to parting. If so, it must be a "reluctant parting," just as Paul and Peter experienced despite their attempts to avoid a division among the Jews and the Gentile Christians.

The eschatological hope for the world by a truly evangelical catholic form of Methodism may remain just that—a hope for a future time. At best, it must always be a vision of what we grow toward, or which hovers over our unhappy divisions as judgment on our limitations and finite structures. As in the letter to the church at Ephesus, we are to "lead a life worthy of the calling to which you have been called, with all humility and gentleness, with patience, bearing with one another in love, making every effort to maintain the unity of the Spirit in the bond of peace" (Eph. 4:1-4, NRSV). We are to "grow up in every way into ... Christ, from whom the whole body, joined and knit together by every ligament (gifts for ministry!) with which it is equipped, as each part is working properly, promotes the body's growth in building itself up in love" (Eph. 4:15-16).

My own limited point of view tells me that, despite the weaknesses of our church institutions, God is still lavishly communicating through the sacraments, through every act of mercy, and in every child awakened to a way of life in Christ. It is true, when a child is born, we cannot tell whether or not the child will be gay or lesbian, for example.

The church should not be in the business of prejudging. After all, the Word "became flesh and lived among us ... full of grace and truth" (John 1:14). For me, this is the heart of the matter. We need a deeper theology. The practices of baptism and the Eucharist make the incarnation of God in Christ visible, audible, and palpable in our denominational ordering of faith and life.

Our mission is surely worldwide, and uniformity as a structured denomination must grow into a way that best serves that mission. Here, we must ask what constitutes membership, representation, and "authority" in the complex relationship between annual conferences, jurisdictional conferences, and the present conception of a "central conference." Perhaps the designation of The United Methodist Church in the United States as the "central conference" would address some of the more political aspects of voting and representation. We still, however, would face serious divisions among us because of deep disagreements.

For my part, scripture and tradition have authority when they address contemporary denial of human dignity in whatever forms. The authority comes from the indelible hesed of God in Christ. The divine "loving-kindness" supersedes human party-spirit. Such love is always and everywhere at work in all attempts to be faithful.

## Postscript

What song shall we sing that comprehends the glory of God and the lamentability of our human world of power, oppression, and unhappy divisions? Suppose that God has given the church, and to Methodist traditions specifically, a song that we slowly learn to sing in our time. It is a baptismal and eucharistic hymn. It is a song of faith, wisdom, and fidelity. John and Charles Wesley did not join in a fractious debate about homosexuality (though they certainly held "traditional" views), but they gave us a wondrous image to sing and live into. We are to be, in Charles' words, "transcriptions of the Trinity." For me, that means, we are called, as a faithful community gathered by Jesus Christ, to mirror the triune life of God in mutuality and in life for the sake of the world, even if Methodism is forced to a reluctant parting.

## One Further Note

One further note on cultural images of homosexuality. Many who find it impossible to conceive of lesbian or gay leadership carry destructive images from our culture (for example, exploitation of these images in film, TV, advertising and, of course, in blatant pornographic industries). Without personal relationships with people in the LGBTQIA+ community, these cultural images play a disturbing and destructive role in forming our convictions and reinforcing prejudices already in place. It is easy to project the degradation of such images before we come to know real people.

**Dr. Don E. Saliers** returned to Candler in 2014 as Theologian-in-Residence after retiring in 2007 as the William R. Cannon Distinguished Professor of Theology and Worship. For many years he directed the Master of Sacred Music program at Emory, and was an organist and choirmaster at Cannon Chapel for 35 years. Before joining the Candler faculty in 1974, Saliers taught at Yale Divinity School, and has taught in summer programs at Notre Dame, Boston College, Vancouver School of Theology, St. John's University, and Boston University School of Theology.

Saliers is the author of 15 books on the relationship between theology and worship practices, as well as more than 150 articles, essays, chapters in books and book reviews. He co-authored *A Song to Sing, a Life to Live* with his daughter Emily Saliers, a member of the band, Indigo Girls.

# CHAPTER TWENTY-ONE
# Amy Valdez Barker
Reconsider the Methodist Mission

## The Syrophoenician Woman

> [21] Jesus went away from there and withdrew into the
> district of Tyre and Sidon. [22] And a Canaanite woman
> from that region came out and began to cry out, saying,
> "Have mercy on me, Lord, Son of David; my daughter is
> cruelly demon-possessed." [23] But He did not answer her a
> word. And His disciples came and implored Him, saying,
> "Send her away, because she keeps shouting [at us]." [24] But
> He answered and said, "I was sent only to the lost sheep
> of the house of Israel." [25] But she came and began to bow
> down before Him, saying, "Lord, help me!" [26] And He
> answered and said, "It is not good to take the children's
> bread and throw it to the dogs." [27] But she said, "Yes,
> Lord; but even the dogs feed on the crumbs which fall
> from their masters' table." [28] Then Jesus said to her, "O
> woman, your faith is great; it shall be done for you as
> you wish." And her daughter was healed at once.

**Matthew 15:21-28, NASB**

Tanzania. Home to the Serengeti, Mt. Kilimanjaro, the Masai
people, and just last year the site for the World Mission Evangelism
Conference. The theme of the event, sponsored by the World Council of Churches, was "Moving in the Spirit: Called to Transforming
Discipleship." The Conference offered participants ways to think
about the incredible variety of missions and ministries that take
place in the margins of life. There were many meetings, worship
services, and bible studies as part of this event.

As I was looking for closing words for a recent meeting, I stumbled upon a Bible study lesson from the Conference that highlighted and offered a unique approach to understanding this particular passage that stood out to me in a striking way. It invited readers to observe the experience between Jesus and this Syrophoenician woman from an outsider's perspective. The Bible study author claimed that this woman "evangelized Jesus." Now many Christians might say, "How on earth could SHE, a woman with no status in society, 'evangelize Jesus?'" Isn't Jesus the one who was evangelizing the world? But, from an outside observer's point of view, this woman (a nobody in most people's eyes) made Jesus STOP and reconsider his mission. Here he tells her, I'm here for the "lost sheep of the house of Israel," and clearly this woman was not a member of this house, so she had no right to access God the way the Israelites did. That didn't stop her. She kept pressing. This Syrophoenician woman didn't deserve his time or attention and was nothing but a nuisance to the disciples and to Jesus. And yet, she dared to press on, letting go of her own pride and decency and lowering herself to the status of an animal, reminding him, "even the dogs feed on the crumbs which fall from their masters' table." It wasn't her status that gained her favor in Christ's eyes. It wasn't her position in the house of Israel. It wasn't even her eloquence in knowing the law. It was the absolute love and devotion for her daughter that pressed her forward to simply plea to Jesus, asking him to reconsider his mission. The author of this Bible study led me to understand the Syrophoenician woman's love healed her daughter and her faith gave renewed hope to Jesus. This emphasis was new to me though the passage was not.

You see, I had learned something previously about this passage while researching for a sermon. Commentators suggested that Jesus was at a low time in his ministry, and he was trying to figure out how to navigate this human place of humility and pride. He knew that the people were not getting his stories and his messages. In fact, the previous story in Matthew 15 reminds us how the Pharisees and the law experts were challenging everything Jesus said and everything his disciples were doing. I can imagine how frustrated he must have been, constantly attacked by the "experts," while knowing he had a gift of knowledge that no one else held. Some commentators said the reason this passage was so significant was because this woman's pure love for her daughter and pure hope in Jesus brought him out of his own frustrations. Her faithfulness lifted him back into a greater mission beyond the house of Israel. In this passage, Jesus, the Son of God, our Savior and Strength, was called to reconsider his mission.

If Jesus can be invited to reconsider his mission, then The

United Methodist Church can as well. Let's just be honest and confess many of us feel like our church is at a whole new level of low in this moment of our ministry together. We have failed to find a way forward that unites us for God's mission and ministry, and if anything, we've doubled down on our differences. My heart is broken.

However, there are many voices out in the world, our mission field, representing the Syrophoenician woman. There are parents who are so in love with their children that they are willing to do anything to get Jesus' attention. These are parents of LGBTQIA+ children, African children, Russian children, Asian children, Latin children, European children, American children, and every child who is in need of God's love and grace. We have got to listen to these voices who are asking The United Methodist Church to reconsider our mission.

Our mission as The United Methodist Church has been about *making disciples of Jesus Christ for the transformation of the world* and there are millions of children out there who are lost, broken, and desperate for healing. We must consider that *the local churches are the most significant arena through which this disciple making occurs* and as a connection, we can strengthen the impact that local churches are making to offer Christ's healing for these children. The problem is, our polity has become entirely too much like the disciples in this story. Our polity has become like the disciples complaining, "send her away, she's nothing but a nuisance to us." Our United Methodist polity has disabled the voice of the Syrophoenician woman and as a result, our UMC is losing hope in our connection and we, United Methodist members, have lost our love for one another.

Our polity has shifted over time and we have emphasized the wrong things. Our polity has put the emphasis on "power and authority," by trying to create equality through voting that never existed and cannot exist in this bureaucratic church system. It moved us out of the realm of relationships and into the realm of democracy, a government institution, not a spiritual institution. When I travel the world and experience the beauty of our diversity in mission, I see the gifts that relationships in Jesus Christ can offer us when Jesus is our center and the love of our neighbor is the mission. But, when we put people into a human system of political structures that places "power" over people, we lose sight of our true mission, which is to bring people into a closer relationship with Jesus Christ.

Some have said to me there is no other way to deal with our differences except through our General Conference political structure. I adamantly disagree. It is crystal clear to me that there are much better ways for us to be the Body of Christ than through the General Conference as it is presently structured. It is also crystal clear to me that we have much to learn about how to make decisions in community and in relationship from people in many other parts of the world rather than a broken political system called General Conference.

The Syrophoenician woman was after a better way of living for her and her daughter. She wanted to be close to Jesus and to have Jesus acknowledge her so her daughter would experience his healing grace. This woman knew if she used the proper channels of authority, like the disciples or the political structures of power, she would never get to Jesus. It didn't take a vote of the disciples for her to experience this gift of grace. If it had, her daughter would have never been healed. It took Jesus' momentary pause to reconsider his mission and her faithfulness. Because of that, she had the opportunity to remind him that even those who are considered as nothing in that world, in that time and place, were in need of his love and grace.

My friends, if it matters at all, it's time for The United Methodist Church to reconsider our mission. Let us not be like the disciples who will allow our polity to send the Syrophoenician woman away. There are practical solutions which many believe will unlock our thinking if we are willing to listen to the voices on the edges and make room for those who are considered unworthy at our tables, giving her more than just the crumbs, offering them instead the full and fulfilling banquet of Jesus our risen Christ. Let's roll up our sleeves and get at this as Jesus would, pausing and listening to the faith of the Syrophoenician woman.

That's where we are right now, getting ready to roll up our sleeves and get to work. Here's where I believe we should go from here.

It has become clear to me that we are in need of an operational change and an attitude change in The United Methodist Church. As noted above, a democratic system of voting on what we believe and what we value with 800-1,000 people isn't pulling us into a greater relationship with one another and with our Creator. Therefore, our connectional system needs to be reconsidered in light of these questions:

1. What kind of connection brings us closer to Christ?

2. What kind of connectional system will bring us closer to one another?

Although we as a church have been striving towards more equity in our polity and in our structures, we have to admit that our history and our attitudes still reflect a colonial way of thinking about our governance and our mission. I know I will offend some with this statement, but because of what I have seen and heard in the various circles I have travelled and participated in our beloved connection, I believe this reflects an existing attitude amongst The United Methodist people. I also want people to note that I believe this need for an attitude change is not just for our Western European and North American UMC members, but it also needs to happen amongst all of our Central Conference UMC members throughout the world. Our history has taught us to have the attitude where we expect the Western Europeans and North Americans to provide the financial resources for the entire connection. And historically, it was accepted and even expected. There were a few churches in Africa and the Philippines and because of their countries' economic circumstances, Western Europeans and North Americans were happy to help make them better communities by trying to make them just like the blessed churches in Western Europe and North America, the US church in particular. I think we can all agree that it was a colonial mindset that had been passed down from generation to generation and the church leaders/members were just carrying forth what they believe was their expected legacy. But everyone knows the mission field has changed and people have been challenging this understanding about mission and ministry more aggressively throughout the world. Books like *When Helping Hurts*,[1] and conferences like the World Mission and Evangelism Conference have shown us that God is working in and through the people even in the margins of our society. Since this isn't a book on our history, I'll stop there and encourage you to take the time to really look into our past so you'll see why I'm making the recommendations for a different attitude and a different polity for the future. The voices like the Syrophoenician woman have been calling out to us for decades and now we must seriously stop and reconsider our Methodist Mission.

As the former top executive of The Connectional Table of The United Methodist Church and the current Executive Director of the unit in Global Ministries responsible for the five regional offices around the world, I believe I have a unique perspective for offering this observation. In my previous role I studied all the General

---

[1] A book written by Steve Corbett and Brian Fikkert about "alleviating poverty and suffering without hurting the poor and yourself" written in 2009. Corbett, Steve and Brian Fikkert, *When Helping Hurts* (Chicago: Moody Publishers, 2009).

Conference mandated committees' work that attempted to give the denomination several options for reconsidering our governance and our collective mission. Over and over again, smart, experienced leaders kept pointing to the need for a different way of relating to one another by offering to get rid of Central Conferences and creating a collection of Jurisdictions around the world.[2] Committees tried to emphasize the need for the US becoming its own Jurisdictional Conference equivalent to others around the world, but the fear over this idea was that it was too intertwined with the homosexuality issue.   Now with General Conference 2019 over, it is even more obvious that the need for a different way of relating is pressing, and for some it will be because of the homosexuality issue and for others it will be because our cultures and our contexts are so different. For me, it is the latter. I believe in unity amid diversity, but not unity through polity. I believe in unity as beloved Children of God and I want to belong and be a part of a church that can see the beauty of God's creation in each and every individual I meet, whether they think like me or not. At the end of the day, I want to be sure that those who call ourselves United Methodist are willing to love like Jesus taught us to love, and live with God's grace at the center of how we operate in this world. This would mean that it's not about the polity, but rather it's about the relationships with all of God's people.

What does a connection based on relationships look like, practically? It's going back to the hard work that was done by many of these committees and pulling out the pure essentials. The essentials are already codified in our UMC *Book of Discipline*. Parts I-IV all capture the heart of our UMC DNA, reminding us of our history, the essence of our relationship models with annual conferences as the central part of our connection, our doctrinal standards, and our theological task. It reminds us of our belief of the "Ministry of All Christians." Part II has been attempting to give the foundations of our Global Nature, which needs to be simplified to express the importance of each annual conference around the world and to figure out how to live out these principles in their own cultures and contexts. When we worked on this at the Connectional Table, we believed that the primary relationships were in the local church and in the annual conference. This is where the hard discussions really need to take place, because this is where people are in relationship with one another.

When you see someone every week, building a relationship

---

[2] This was a recommendation by one of the first Worldwide Nature Study Committee report led by Bishop Jones.

on the day-to-day details of life, it is much harder to reject them because of their lifestyle. Whether it is someone who is gay, has gay family members, or who is in a polygamous relationship, when you serve this person communion or pass the peace to them, when you look into their eyes you understand a little bit of their journey each time. This is where grace is understood and practiced each and every day in our churches across the world. Jesus couldn't just ignore the woman who was begging at his feet. He had to face her, listen to her, and see her pleading eyes to understand her need for God's healing and grace.

> *"Hard conversations should only happen in these contexts, not in the political body of General Conference where the clergy delegates across the world only see each other every four years."*

Amongst clergy relationships, the annual conference is the central body responsible for the accountability of those called to ministry. It is in these annual gatherings where clergy leaders are positioned to see one another, check-in with one another, and truly be with each other in every day ministry, all these are times and places where we can truly hold one another accountable in love. This is why the annual conference is the primary body of the connection. Hard conversations about those "fit for ministry," should only happen in these contexts, not in the political body of General Conference where the clergy delegates across the world only see each other every four years, IF they were lucky enough to get elected again by their colleagues. How can they truly be in relationship with one another to know what the mission field needs for people "fit for ministry?"

In other words, laity and clergy need to understand their direct neighbors' needs. General Conference does not need to be the body who determines what "fit for ministry" looks like in every context and every region around the world. General Conference does not need to be the body who determines how local churches extend grace and love and accompany people living on the edges of their own societies. This work needs to be done in the places where the relationships are created, cultivated, and nurtured daily, weekly. and annually. Our system has already allowed for that by giving authority and freedom to both local churches and annual conferences in many matters of mission. Why not give that latitude in all matters of ministry and mission?

That would mean that the *General Book of Discipline* for the whole United Methodist Church would be limited to just the pure essentials. It would mean that the book would become less than a hundred pages so that it can be easily translated and communicated throughout the connection. By doing this, we put the missional responsibilities back in the hands of the people who have to live the mission in context day in and day out in the places where God has planted them. The rest of the *Discipline* becomes ideas for sharing how different annual conferences have organized to meet their missional needs. The Standing Committee on Central Conference Matters is offering an idea of having these other non-essentials become "Operating Manuals or Handbooks" for mission and ministry. It would simplify the complexity of our structure and once again save the toughest decisions for where people are in the closest relationships. Yes, it may be difficult, but people can live in greater hope with one another, when they really know and understand the lives of each other. Again, back to the Syrophoenician woman, Jesus made a decision that the disciples didn't like, but because he was right there with them, he could help them understand why he chose to reconsider his mission and why it was important to offer this woman hope. Tough decisions need to be made, but they can't be made over ten days with people who don't know one another and don't have to walk with each other in their everyday ministry settings. Each culture around the world has a culturally relevant way of dealing with conflict in their local settings. In Africa, it's coming to the river or sitting under the palaver tree. In other places, it's the conferences and retreats. No matter what place it is, conflict is best resolved when people are in direct relationship with one another, constantly coming together to better understand each other. General Conference is not a system that allows for conflicts to be resolved through relationships and, therefore, it needs to change.

I know this simple idea that I'm putting out there does lead to more questions like, "Would the operational manuals be created in the Annual Conference, Jurisdiction, or Central Conference?" "What about the social principles? Do they belong as decisions for the annual conference, too?" Or, "What would happen to our General Agencies and the apportionment systems? Where do all the billions of dollars of current assets in our Global Connection go?" And, for me, this is where our human nature of greed and power begin to get back in the way. As they say, the devil is in the details.

A colleague of mine recently went to a meeting of a group of US Annual Conference leaders and he said they were all willing to walk away from our current polity and start something fresh and new. But one comment pulled them back to our human tendencies when he said, "Yeah, but what about those billions of dollars of assets?" Simply put, both sides are interestingly preoccupied about who gets the money and both sides aren't quite ready to give that up. In fact, I have heard that they are gearing up for 2020 to "win at all costs." Jesus didn't come to our world to have people be divided and torn away from each other and from God. Christ came to bring people closer to one another and closer to the Creator. If we can get past this, then we can focus back in on people who are like the Syrophoenician woman, begging for Jesus' attention to save her daughter. When we listen to those people, then I believe that we will not be stopped by anything, like the lack of resources, lack of systems, or lack of structures, to answer the Holy Spirit's call. We will connect with one another to offer God's saving grace to the people who are in need.

My experiences in mission and ministry have reminded me that people in developing countries primary need is not money. Their primary need is to have connections: connections to other people who are willing to teach them new trades, willing to show them how to use the land that they already possess, and offer them hope of a life beyond war, because they are fully gifted and skilled to lift themselves out of poverty with the power of the Holy Spirit. The Holy Spirit uses people in connection to bring them new ideas, new innovations, and hope because they are not alone.

We need to stop believing that money will solve their problems. That's the primary attitude change that starts us toward a new day. The Syrophoenician wasn't asking for money, she was asking for Jesus' time. She wanted Jesus to see her, and recognize her, as more valuable than the dogs who beg at the master's table. She wanted Jesus to give her just a moment of his time so that she might claim hope and validate her faith in the possibilities that God could do in her life. And at the end of the day, it was her faith that healed her daughter.

I need to believe that it will not be our complex polity or millions of dollars of assets or even our bishops and delegates to General Conference who will save God's work through The United Methodist Church. I believe that it will be the good and faithful people in the local churches who are wanting to learn from one another, listen to one another, and even reach out to each other across millions of miles to connect with one another. These are the people who will teach and show us what it looks like to reconsider the Methodist Mission. They are already doing this even without the complex polity of The UMC telling them what to do or how to do it. Yes, there are parts of the connection that enhance the mission, but let's pare it down to the bare essentials and get centered back in our mission. Mission is messy and we've got to live through the messes together and turn it into a message, as one colleague reminded me. Wesley said, "In essentials unity, in non-essentials diversity, and in all things charity." This is how we can reconsider the Methodist Mission today.

**Amy Valdez Barker** leads a staff that relates to partners in the worldwide United Methodist and ecumenical mission network, seeking to foster collaborative interaction for church development and Christian service. She has extensive experience on the connectional level of the church, having worked for the Connectional Table, a program and policy coordinating agency, from 2010 to 2017, four years as the top executive. She served as a Board member of four General Agencies (GCORR, GCFA, GBCS and GCOM) between 1987 and 2003. She also served as a member of the World Methodist Council Executive Committee when she was fifteen years old. Amy is the author of *Trust By Design: The Beautiful Behaviors of an Effective Church Culture* (Abingdon).

Amy is an ordained deacon in the North Georgia Annual Conference. She did her undergraduate study at University of Iowa in Communication Studiesand has earned both a Masters degree and PhD from Garrett Evangelical Theological Seminary.

# CHAPTER TWENTY-TWO
# Laceye C. Warner

United Methodism: A Church Disconnected

## Losing Connection

There has been much discussion about the current difficulties in The United Methodist Church around issues arising from the church's stance on ordination and marriage of LGBTQIA+ persons. Some see the stance as a moral failing to stand up for justice. Others frame the argument as a struggle to uphold the authority of scripture. Certainly, there is an air of palpable tension about the future of the church on all sides. This particular issue has scythed through mainline Protestantism, and it seems like the UMC is the next group to experience schism over these important questions and relationships.

Division within the UMC was made more tangible by the recent vote to support intensified restrictions on LGBTQIA+ persons seeking ordination and marriage. On Tuesday afternoon February 26, 2019, the Traditional Plan prevailed with a vote of 438 to 384 passing legislation to further limit, monitor, and prevent access to ordination and forbid clergy to marry anyone beyond heterosexual couples. For most, this is not surprising since it reflects cultural divisions in the United States. As many realize, the compulsive and seemingly unstoppable cycle of pain and trauma is devastating to individuals and communities on all sides.

While many ruminate on the damage inflicted by such divisive debates, as well as the macro trends fueling them, the simplicity behind the UMC's deep incision is stunning. Sitting at tables with conservative delegates while voting, and talking with centrists, moderates, and progressives over meals, the difference in goals, language, culture, and response is stark. The two sides that inevitably galvanized hold tightly to different goals, described in distinct languages, and embodied in different world views.

I would argue our current failing is less about justice and scripture (though these in principle are among the highest of our aspirations as Christians) and infinitely more ordinary. I offer that The United Methodist Church is experiencing a crisis of the most basic sort - connection. Certainly, it is possible for committed, faithful Christians to disagree with one another, and to disagree deeply and passionately. John Wesley's guidance on which are the core issues that we must all agree, and on the lesser issues we can think and let think, holds open the possibility for such disagreements to exist within the larger body. Of course, what are core issues and what are lesser issues is a more difficult conversation. It is our relationships, characterized by trust, rather than suspicion, embodied in our governance which allows the UMC, or any organization, to sort out what to do when different opinions are deeply held. Unfortunately, in the current circumstances, the UMC's networks and systems are disintegrating. In the language of John Wesley, 'United Methodists no longer seem to live in or practice connexion.'

Our church structures are predicated on shared goals, relationships, and networks characterized by trust; after all, we are a church. Currently, the UMC's structure includes little, if any, accountability and very few actual operating procedures. Without presumptions of trust and interpretive charity, the lack of accountability and recognized shared procedures, the UMC is captive to an endless litany of accusations and polemics. In short, we have lost our ability to practice conferencing as a means of grace.

Furthermore, the structure is inhabited by members representing very different cultures. Yes, this includes general conference delegates fluent in numerous first languages requiring translation and orientation to various voting and other technical tools to facilitate communication and organization of such a large gathering. It also includes those within the United States and beyond, with fundamentally disparate goals, language, methods, presuppositions, interpretations, and practices. Indeed, these cultural and ideological particularities at times feature in unintentional, yet deeply disturbing ways. For example, assumptions may be declared about one another's oppression, capitulation, or dominance and coercion without careful attention and openness in sustained conversations with each other. I am struck by the immense number of statements, declaratory and imperative statements, on all sides following the special general conference rather than inquiries.

Sitting on the floor of the Special General Conference at an assigned table of delegates alongside hundreds of other tables of delegates, I was struck by the disparities. Not those characterized by the challenge of linguistic translation and visas or even the obstacle of Robert's Rules, but the deep divides between worldviews, language, and therefore goals of delegates from the same jurisdiction sitting at neighboring tables. Not only are the acceptable methods for preparing for such a monumental gathering in stark difference, but the pernicious and extensive lack of understanding of one another among those from very similar demographics.

As much as I would like to hold on to my anger towards some on all sides, I am moved to compassion and grief for the deep bereavement of our church. Indeed, we made a decision that essentially hurts both sides and all in between, but in essence this decision exposes the divides and mistrust that have deepened over many years, even decades. Conversations with delegates on all sides demonstrate a deep and incisive lack of awareness and understanding of one another. We are not just unpracticed in our holy conferencing, we lack the fundamental relationships, common language, practices, and trust, to even begin to imagine a context of holy conferencing. In this way, there is no legislation or form of governance structures that can assist us.

While the General Conference is the authoritative voice of The United Methodist Church, it, along with other components of our polity, is unable sufficiently to embody a church that has grown so disconnected in its sub-cultures and ideological commitments.

Presently The United Methodist Church maintains a steady, and since the Special General Conference in February 2019 an even swifter, course toward fracture. With the term fracture, I mean to indicate a deep-seated tension and conflict that eventually breaks apart in shards producing the sharpest of edges that there is no human-led recovery possible. At this point, all sides seem indignant, defensive, and inaccessible.

However, there is always hope with our Triune God. If influential thought leaders from the various perspectives could see themselves to a space of contented openness The United Methodist Church may demonstrate the capacity to address the lingering questions and controversies in 2020. That said, the questions of marriage and ordination confronting the denomination represent merely the tip of the iceberg of our disconnection. If this is plausible, the work of reconnecting still remains. Reconnecting would require a non-anxious space to meet one another and accept one another in whatever manner that is possible.

## Reconnecting as Means of Grace?

> "In the meantime let all those who are real members of
> the church see that they walk holy and unblameable in all
> things... Above all things, let your love abound."
>
> **John Wesley**

The church in Wesleyan and Methodist tradition is a *means of grace*. This description from Richard Heitzenrater is in an effort to align the being of the church, or what it "is" and the practices of the church, or what it "does." The means of grace in Wesleyan and Methodist tradition acknowledge the presence and accessibility to God's grace for those participating in individual or communal practices. The church is the place where through worship, prayer, the sacraments, and conferencing, (all considered means of grace by John Wesley) one's understanding of Christian doctrine and its embodiment is formed and challenged. The church at its best functions as a, though not the only, means of God's grace.

The UMC's, among other denominations in the Wesleyan tradition, character as a means of grace includes much, if not all, of its organization and polity alongside worship, sacraments, and ordination. For example, the structure of annual conferences, the episcopacy, and the itineracy, may be understood as prudential means of grace. While these may falter in specific circumstances, throughout its history the formation of the movement's structure has kept its missional purpose at the center.

The language of connection, or *connexion*, dates to usage by John Wesley to describe the character of the early Methodist renewal movement. The early Methodist renewal movement seems to have relied on three convictions according to Brian Beck:

1. Christ died for all (so mission is the primary imperative).

2. All are called to holy living (hence the discipline and the need for oversight).

3. There is no such thing as solitary religion (hence the societies and all that is designed to sustain them).

Wesley used the term *connexion* to refer to at least three layers of relationships within the movement for which he was the center as well as the authority—members, societies, and preachers—with a later addition of the conference. Several pragmatic attributes such as the development of band and class meetings, itineracy, rules, hymns, sermons, and *Notes upon the New Testament* as well as other publications in the Christian library supported this connexion. Eventually, particularly for Methodism in the United States, the trust clause was added, ensuring the ownership and use of facilities would remain held in trust for the annual conference, building upon what are now called doctrinal standards including the Articles of Religion.

In the United States and beyond, Methodist connection continues to represent multiple complex, yet related, themes, predominantly relationships such as itineracy, superintendency, organizational structure from classes to conferences, and discipline, eventually the *Book of Discipline* and worship practices. For Russell Richey, United Methodism institutionalizes three competing structures of connectionalism from Wesley's time: superintendency and appointment-making, legislative decision-making authority of the conference, and organizational work in agencies. In this way and in light of Special General Conference 2019, connectionalism lacks a simplicity and clarity to inform a consistent use of the term and facilitate understanding of the concept it represents.

> *"The purpose is to constantly seek renewal of God's image in persons, communities, and creation through participating in God's mission."*

If United Methodists choose to reclaim practicing our connexion as a means of grace, we are far from holy conferencing. As I teach those seeking credentials for ministry, I am consistently in awe of the simple brilliance of our polity in theory, if not in practice: The sole purpose of our Methodist beliefs (or doctrine), and practice (or polity and governance), is simply to facilitate and define our mission (or participation in God's mission). Historians, and even theologians, can hyper-focus on the many ways we distance ourselves from this simple formula of belief, practices, and mission. The purpose is to constantly seek renewal of God's image in persons, communities, and creation through participating in God's mission.

Following the 2019 Special General Conference, I argue the UMC would benefit immensely from a comprehensive self-examination to describe our current identity in the most honest and transparent ways. This will require suspending judgements for a time, but is necessary to survey our substance and process eventually to assess our viability and sustainability as a body. This will also require attention to questions that do not serve any particular political agenda, set, or section of United Methodists, but rather seeks data that is candidly and refreshingly non-partisan. We know very little about ourselves and each other within the UMC, much less Methodist and Wesleyan connection. If we can suspend judgement and rationale toward implications and consequences, we can honestly examine ourselves in the light of God's love and purpose. Then, together discern what is best for the body, not merely select parts. After self-examination of much, if not all, of our structure and ministry, I encourage us to consider framing and implementing practices of accountability and standard operating procedures across the connection that includes considering post-colonial practices and networks. I could go on, but ultimately the choice to practice deeply honest self-examination and discernment is not solely mine, though I appreciate the opportunity to share these thoughts.

Methodists have continued to speak of ourselves and our church as a connection even after a motion to expunge the language of connection from the Methodist Episcopal *Discipline* at the 1816 General Conference (the first following Frances Asbury's death, en route to the gathering). Richey argues this simple motion may symbolize Methodists' inability and/or lack of desire adequately to draw out the rich implications of their connectionalism either for themselves or for the larger Christian community. At its best, Methodism embodies a connectionalism that is both organizational and functional as well as theological and eschatological, connecting the ministry and mission of the denomination to the unfolding reign of God.

May United Methodists reclaim the practice of connexion as a means of grace so that we may experience and be led by the Holy Spirit to participate in God's mission.

**Laceye Warner** serves as the associate professor of the practice of evangelism and Methodist studies and associate dean of Wesleyan engagement at Duke Divinity School. Dr. Warner taught at Garrett-Evangelical Theological Seminary at Northwestern University as the E. Stanley Jones Assistant Professor of Evangelism. She has served urban congregations in the Methodist Church of Great Britain.

She was a contributing editor to the Wesley Study Bible and completed a co-authored book with Bishop Kenneth Carder entitled *Grace to Lead: Practicing Leadership in the Wesleyan Tradition,* which was published in Fall 2010. Her most recent book is *The Method of Our Mission: United Methodist Polity and Organization,* published by Abingdon Press in 2014. Dr. Warner is the author of numerous reviews and articles for academic and ecclesial audiences and the recipient of scholarly and ecclesial grants. Her teaching areas include theology of evangelism, women's ministry practices, and Methodist/Wesleyan studies.

# CHAPTER TWENTY-THREE
# J.J. Warren

From a long and visceral death comes
a glorious resurrection.

*Though the title of my chapter begins with a tone
of despair, disparity is not my story.*

While I walked the halls of the Special Session of General
Conference, I encountered many people from a variety of countries, languages, perspectives, and ages. I met with the few young
delegates who were elected as we shared our hopes for the UMC.
I walked to worship with United Methodists from the Congo. I
ate with United Methodists from the Philippians. I laughed with
United Methodists from California. I cried with United Methodists
from the U.K. I shouted with United Methodists from Connecticut,
upstate New York, Iowa, and many other areas as we cried out for
justice. I experienced the beauty of our family amidst the pain of
our division.

One encounter in particular has left me with a haunting, yet
convicting, impression. As I left the floor of General Conference to
talk with other reserve delegates and visitors in the stands, I was
stopped by an elderly gray-haired woman. She, like many of us,
wore a rainbow-colored stole and looked at me earnestly. "I've been
coming to these since they started," she said. "I've been fighting to
see us be an inclusive Church since I was your age." I looked into
her eyes and I felt so much grief, but I also felt unwavering resolve.
After a moment of mutual embrace, I looked back into her eyes, and
after another moment, we parted ways.

This woman haunts my memory because in that moment I
wondered, *Will that be me? Will I find myself well-advanced in age,
still yearning to see my Church include me? Will it take that long?
Will I stay that long?* These questions turned over and over in my
mind like the leaves in the harsh wind outside. Perhaps what is
most difficult for me is that deep within my being I know I will stay.
I am convicted to forge forward through this wilderness of pain, to

189

carry our cross and flame through the desert with my fellow queer siblings and allies, to make The United Methodist Church a safe home for all of us—no matter how long it takes. I *will* be that gray-haired, time-worn United Methodist, fighting for inclusion if I have to (though I'd rather not wait that long).

## A Place of Pain

As many of my fellow United Methodist colleagues have said already, we are in a place of pain. As a global denomination we are deeply divided. Our understanding of scripture as it relates to human sexuality has been caught in the crosshairs of a deeper institutional issue: How do we function as a truly global body? Our contexts have shown division, and this division is inflicting harm on the body. A difference of only 54 votes derailed decades of justice work. If anything is clear from this vote, it's that we cannot function as we are. A simple majority cannot be said to discern the will of God. We are a global body which is indeed broken.

Though many well-intentioned United Methodists claim that our decision in St. Louis does not exclude the LGBTQIA+ community, it does. By a slim majority, we voted to continue our decades of exclusion, discrimination, and pain. To these United Methodists who insist that we are welcome, I ask you, *How much are we welcomed?* To be told that we are welcome to worship and pay into the offering, yet kept from serving God in this Church is not only unwelcoming and insulting, it's unjust. As a gay certified candidate for ministry who is about to enter a United Methodist seminary, I face many challenges. My bishop has said he will not ordain me, my BoOM (Board of Ordained Ministry) will not sign a letter of non-compliance, and I've postponed my meeting with my DCOM (District Committee on Ordained Ministry) in hopes of stalling until after the Judicial Council ruling. If my DCOM discontinues my candidacy I will lose my seminary funding. The decision at the Special Session did not welcome me into our Church.

So, when my well-intentioned colleagues say that we have not reinforced our exclusion of LGBTQIA+ persons, I respectfully disagree.

It must be known that LGBTQIA+ youth are *four times more likely* to commit suicide than their straight peers. Why do you think this is?

LGBTQIA+ people and our families have been, and continue to be, harmed by the Church which we have for so long called home. It is not enough to say we are welcomed in the door. We need to be loved for who we are once inside. I wonder how many of those queer teenagers who felt there was no other option than to end their lives attended a church? Some of them must have been United Methodists. Where they truly welcomed into their churches? What did their pastors tell them about their sexuality? What did the congregation say about LGBTQIA+ people? Did they know the child was gay? Did they try to change them or teach them that their love was a sin? What did the kids at youth group say? Did they bully them for being different? Did they feel justified in their bullying?

Lives are being taken because of our struggle to exist as a diverse global body.

## Response to "The Speech"

After I made my speech against separation before the Special Session of General Conference, I received thousands of emails and direct messages on my social media platforms. Many of these messages were from parents of queer children who were thankful to know that there are others like their children, other queer people who are committed to God and to The United Methodist Church. Several mothers sent photos of their children and asked that we keep fighting for our Church to be a safe place for them. One mother sent me a photo of her twelve-year-old daughter standing next to a gay flag which was newly added to their church entrance.

> "Because of your testimony, and the testimonies of many like you, my little country church decided to openly say that we celebrate LGBTQIA+ people. My daughter felt comfortable today in worship to come out to our church and to our family. Thank you."

Another message I received was from a self-defined conservative United Methodist from Germany. His message read as follows:

> "I have to say that I am one of 'those' traditionalists. And I really do not write this mail to have any kind of discussion, but I write because I felt sorry for many words that people like me said to people like you. I want to ask you for forgiveness, were ever I judged people from the LGBTQI community to not understand and not respekt [sic] the scripture."

He continued,

> "I learned while watching the GC and some videos of your YouTube channel, that you love the Bible, you love

the people and you really try hard, much more than I do,
to spread the love of God among the world and to bring
people into a relationship with Jesus, no matter how and
who they are... I have noticed that I have to open my eyes
even more and I'd like to hear your experience of being gay
and Christian."

What this United Methodist did is one of the reasons why I am
willing to remain in our UMC family, even if that means fighting
until I, too, am gray-haired. This man listened. Unlike the protest-
ers from Westboro Baptist Church who spat condemnations in the
form of Scripture, this United Methodist listened, and he understood
that I respect Scripture as well.

He heard from the words on my heart that I, too, love God. He
was willing to set aside his personal convictions about how to interpret Scripture so that he could truly listen. And when he did, his
heart was strangely warmed, and upon reading his email, my heart
was warmed as well.

We are a broken body, but we are not finished.

## A Facebook Message

I received a Facebook message from a teenager this morning. It
said, "Thank you for what you said at General Conference. Because
of that, I decided to become a member of my UMC."

Many within the UMC are understandably exhausted of fighting.
They're tired of focusing on Church policies rather than on sharing the Gospel. The work which we do around the world matters.
While you read this book, the UM Committee on Relief is working
in over 60 countries around the world, and in every U.S. state, to
provide disaster response, agricultural education, and healthcare.
The General Board of Higher Education and Ministry is overseeing
thirteen UM seminaries, educating and equipping thousands of
young leaders for the work of Christ. Africa University is providing
jobs and pastoral training to previously untouched areas, creating
access to education and aiding the local economy. UM clergy are
laying down their lives in protest along the U.S.-Mexico border to
bring awareness to the ill treatment of our southern friends. UM
Churches are providing free meals to thousands of hungry folks,
and our youth are gathering in masses to share their passion for
God in an increasingly secular age. What would happen to all of
these people if we ceased to exist?

I believe that the story of our UMC is not over. Yes, we have experienced great pain, but this pain can lead to a glorious resurrection,

if we are willing to cooperate with each other in new ways.

The teenager who messaged me felt convicted that the UMC could one day be a safe space for him to be nurtured spiritually. The conservative German was willing to admit the harm that his convictions have caused me and others like me, and he wanted to remain in relationship together. Young United Methodists from Norway and the Philippines reached out to me expressing how desperately they desire our Church to remain together. Though our global body has inflicted much harm, we are blessed by the unique gifts of each member of this body. The world truly is our parish. Now, it's time to care for our sheep.

*"We are a deeply divided Church, and it would be naïve of me to think that we will soon settle our disputes."*

I am convinced that we must move forward together as a global body which strives to share the love of Christ with the world because we do so in transformative ways. I am convinced that our Wesleyan heritage has much to offer the world. I am convinced that we must be in relationship with our global siblings through the gift of our UM connection. I am convinced that our Church must also be transformed. Robert's Rules of Order do not allow room for the movement of the Holy Spirit to warm hearts through loving dialogue. Our global structuring must change. The U.S. must end its continued colonialism by influencing other parts of the globe, and the U.S. must itself become a central conference. We must allow for contextuality and we must not hold back the Spirit of God in some places because it has yet to move others.

We are a deeply divided Church, and it would be naïve of me to think that we will soon settle our disputes. I'm reminded of the prime directive from Star Trek: we must not interfere with the evolution of other cultures. While I know that God has created and loves LGBTQIA+ persons, I realize that in many of countries in which the UMC ministers, homosexual acts are against the law. These laws are unjust and despicable, yet we are faced with a moral dilemma. Do we exert our understanding of what is just, and thereby continue our colonialism, or do we allow time for these cultures to have this debate on their own? I truly do not know.

What I do know is that we must all have the freedom to follow God's Spirit of justice, and we must be enabled to remain in relationship with our global family. What has died is not The United Methodist Church altogether, but rather, the flawed structuring of our institution. We have seen the failure of our current structure to represent the majority of United Methodist voices in the U.S., in Germany, and in our affiliated churches. The UMC, as it has been structured, must finally be taken off the cross after its brutal beatings in St. Louis. We must lay this body in the tomb and search for the risen truth of Christ.

I am convicted to remain a United Methodist, and I am convicted that we will find a way forward together toward God's inclusive love. I hope you will remain in this family as well.

**J.J. Warren** is currently a senior at Sarah Lawrence College, just outside New York City, and is a certified candidate for ministry in The United Methodist Church. J.J. spent the 2017-18 academic year studying Biblical Hebrew and theology at Oxford University, England. During summer 2018, J.J. had his first preaching tour, "Renewal," in which he was invited to speak at eight churches in seven weeks around the state of New York.

J.J. has spent the past four years preaching at churches and youth events, founding a progressive Christian community on his campus, leading the Young Adult Ministries Team of the Upper NY Conference, and was a lay delegate to the Special Session of the General Conference in February, where he made an impassioned speech for inclusion and unity, which was featured by the Huffington Post.

Market
Square
BOOKS

**marketsquarebooks.com**

Clergy leaders in the most religiously challenging region of the U.S., often referred to as the "None Zone," offer testimonies and evidence of ministries that speak to the changing realities of 21st century society.

# FILLING THE VOID

The decline of church membership in the United States is a complex issue. While it is right and appropriate to question whether or not the ministries of the church continue to be relevant for this time and age, it is equally important to recognize the changing face of the America. Changing demographics have made the United States a much more ethnically, culturally, and religiously pluralistic society than ever before. In addition, the explosion of urban centers has made life more economically complex and challenging with a concomitant impact on religious life and involvement. In spite of these realities, while the church is on the decline, it is far from dead.

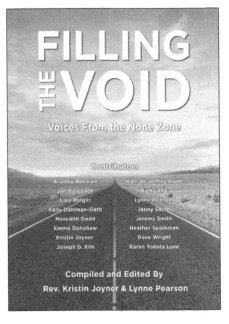

The narratives of these clergy leaders in the most religiously challenging region of the United States, the Pacific Northwest, often referred to as the "None Zone," offer testimonies and evidence of vibrant church life and ministries that speak to the changing realities of 21st century society. As Reverend Rich Lang, the District Superintendent of the SeaTac Missional District, reminds us, the "None Zone" can be an "Abundant Zone," and he is seeing "true abundance in congregations that are learning to build relational partnerships with others who share their values."

The stories each of these pastors share are powerful. Their experiences can become best practices for the revival of religiosity and church life, not only in the "None Zone" of the Pacific Northwest but also in other regions of the United States.

Bradley Beeman • Jan Bolerjack • Lara Bolger • Kelly Dahlman-Oeth
Meredith Dodd • Emma Donohew • Kristin Joyner • Joseph D. Kim
Kah-Jin Jeffrey Kuan • Rich Lang • Lynne Pearson • Jenny Smith
Jeremy Smith • Heather Sparkman • Dave Wright • Karen Yokota Love

NEW TITLES FROM

# Market Square Books

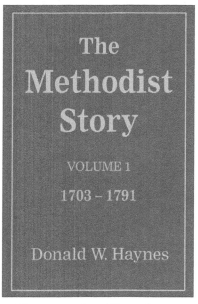

## Mission Possible
### *A Simple Structure for Missional Effectiveness*

**By Kay Kotan & Blake Bradford**

This book will lead you through both the technical and adaptive shifts that will need to be addressed to align your church to the mission of making disciples. If you came to this book looking for only the technical "how-to's" for moving into simplified structure so you can have fewer meetings, you may be a bit frustrated. Our intention is to challenge you to move beyond making this just a technical change, but to also move you through this very large adaptive change. It is in the adaptive change that churches can create a whole new trajectory of vitality with a deeper impact.

If you are ready to partake in a bold, brave journey for you and your church towards faithfulness in fruitful ministries, let the journey begin!

## The Methodist Story
## Volume 1: 1703-1791

**By Dr. Donald W. Haynes**

"Dr. Haynes has pulled together the thinking of many of the finest minds that have tackled the developing spirit of Wesley and put them into a masterful narrative. We all grow as Wesley did during his long life, and perhaps in the end we are a bit closer to understanding each other within the Wesleyan scheme."

**Richard P. Heitzenrater**
The Divinity School, Duke University

"Few people have been shaped by more themes that make up the fabric of United Methodism's past and promise than this author. The story he tells is about history, but it also comes from the heart."

**Lovett H. Weems, Jr.**
Wesley Theological Seminary, Washington, DC

# Other Books

## from Market Square

marketsquarebooks.com

## Hear It, See It, Risk It
How Faith Grows

Steve Cordle

## A Digest of
## Wesleyan Grace Theology

Donald W. Haynes

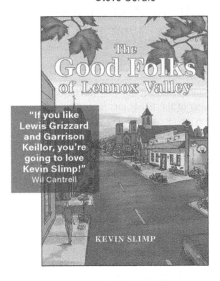

## The Good Folks
## of Lennox Valley

Kevin Slimp

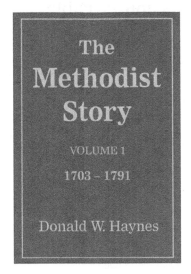

## The Methodist Story
## 1792-2019

Donald W. Haynes

# Grow Your Faith

## with these books from Market Square

marketsquarebooks.com

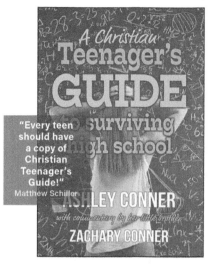

**A Christian Teenager's Guide
to Surviving High School**

Ashley Conner

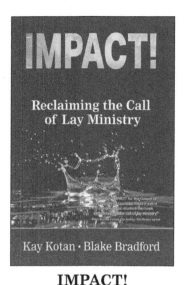

**IMPACT!**
*Reclaiming the Call of Lay Ministry*

Kay Kotan & Blake Bradford

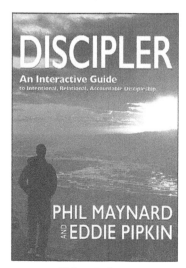

**Discipler**

Phil Maynard & Eddie Pipkin

**Understanding Your Call**

*Perhaps these eleven Biblical figures
can help you understand your call*

# Practical Guides for Leaders

## with these books from Market Square

marketsquarebooks.com

**Obvious Wisdom**

Bishop Bob Farr

**Coming Fall '19**

From Franchise to Local Drive

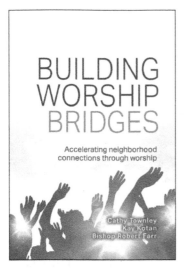

**Building Worship Bridges**

Cathy Townley

**Get Out of That Box!**

Anne Bosarge